W9-AET-424

READING
BUDDHIST ART

READING
BUDDHIST ART

An Illustrated Guide to Buddhist Signs and Symbols

MEHER McARTHUR

With 304 illustrations

Thames & Hudson

Art is what reveals to us the state of perfection
Shingon Buddhist Priest, Kobo Daishi, Japan, ninth century

This book is dedicated to those who seek
spiritual perfection through the arts

Opposite title page:
Avalokiteshvara emerging from
stupa (detail), thangka painting in
colors on silk, Tibet, c. 1700

First published in hardcover in the United States of America in 2002 by
Thames & Hudson Inc., 500 Fifth Avenue, New York, New York 10110

thamesandhudsonusa.com

Library of Congress Catalog Card Number 2001099696
ISBN 0-500-51089-x

Printed and bound in Singapore by Star Standard Industries

Contents

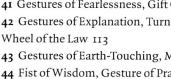

SECTION III

Major Buddhist Sites

First, I would like to thank Jamie Camplin of Thames & Hudson for recognizing the need for a basic guide to the arts of Buddhism and for helping to develop its structure. For his support in this project and for the loan of so many images from Pacific Asia Museum, I would like to thank David Kamansky, Executive Director and Senior Curator of Pacific Asia Museum, Pasadena, California. I would also like to thank Robert E. Fisher, David Kamansky and Sally McKay for taking time out of their busy schedules to read over the text and suggest improvements; and John Listopad and Kim Thanh Bui for help with Thai and Vietnamese terms, Youngsook Park and Kim Bokyung for help with Korean terms and Steve Conroy for help with Chinese terms. I extend both gratitude and admiration to Carol Fulton for her superb line drawings of Buddhist figures and symbols, which will be of tremendous assistance to readers. For her invaluable help in organizing the images for the book, I would like to thank my enthusiastic and hard-working assistant, Sian Leong.

I am also grateful to the Norton Simon Museum, the Los Angeles County Museum of Art and Santa Barbara Museum of Art for lending images from their collection, and to Sam Fogg and Emma Henderson of Sam Fogg, London for lending images of Japanese Buddhist art. I am grateful also to the John C. and Susan L. Huntington Photographic Archive of Buddhist & Related Arts at the Ohio State University for providing images from their remarkable archive. In addition, I would like to thank Alan Bair, Virgil Bryant, Kendall H. Brown, the Chagdud Gonpa Foundation of Los Angeles, David Humphrey, Pat and Bill Johnston, Alan McArthur, Sandra Sheckter, Tools for Peace, Los Angeles, Leslie Rinchen Wongmo (for providing images of her exquisite pieced silk appliqué works) and Tsunemitsu Yajima (for Monya Art Co.), Ruth Hayward and Tom Grayson for providing many fine photographs of Buddhist sites or of their own Buddhist works of art. I would like to offer special thanks to Julian Bermudez for photographing the many images from the collection of Pacific Asia Museum.

Finally, I would like to express my love and gratitude to David Marsh and my family and friends who have supported and encouraged me throughout this project.

Preface

Buddhist art is not the product of one single, unified belief system. Nor is it the product of one nation or culture. Buddhism has a history of over 2,500 years, and its arts have existed for almost as long, weaving their way with monks and pilgrims across broad areas of the Asian continent and across seas, intermingling with the existing arts and styles of the cultures they encountered. Not surprisingly, the teachings and imagery of this international religion are complex, and to many students of Buddhism and its arts, the task of deciphering Buddhist iconography and symbolism can seem as challenging as the search for enlightenment itself.

This book is intended as a basic guide to Buddhist iconography and symbolism. It does not attempt to delve into the intricacies of this complex religion. Nor does it attempt to present a chronological or geographical survey of the vast body of art that has been born out of Buddhism over the last two millennia. Instead, it introduces many figures of worship – Buddhas, bodhisattvas, deities, protectors of the faith and historical personages – and explains their origins, characters, identifying features and the areas where they are most commonly worshipped. It also introduces the principal symbols taken to illustrate Buddhist ideas over the centuries, as well as many of the objects used during worship and meditation. Finally, the book explores several major Buddhist sites, with information about their patrons and their principal features.

Wherever possible, the names of the deities, symbols and objects have been given in the languages of the cultures where they are most predominant. In order to ease the reading of many non-English terms, diacritical marks have not been employed.

How to Use this Book

The introduction gives a brief overview of the life of the Buddha, the emergence of Buddhism and its arts in India and the spread of the religion and its arts throughout Asia. The main body of the book is divided into three thematic sections: (1) The Buddhist Pantheon and its Iconography; (2) Buddhist Signs, Symbols and Ritual Objects; (3) Major Buddhist Sites. Each subject is numbered for cross reference, and generally occupies two pages, one with a description and explanation of the subject, the other with illustrations. Many photographs show Buddhist art in situ in temples or in the homes of worshippers; others show objects now in museum or private collections. In addition, two-colour line drawings help to illustrate particular aspects of the figures, symbols or places being discussed. For many of the subjects discussed, their names are given in several languages, mainly Sanskrit, Tibetan, Chinese and Japanese, but occasionally in Thai, Vietnamese and Korean. At the end of the book is a glossary of key Buddhist terms, followed by a guide to further reading and an index.

Buddhism has been one of the world's most successful religions. From its beginnings in India in the sixth century BC, it has travelled from the Indian subcontinent north to the Himalayan regions of Nepal and Tibet, through Central Asia to China, Korea and Japan, and south to Sri Lanka and large areas of Southeast Asia. Although it no longer has a strong presence in the land of its birth, it still thrives in its various forms in many of these areas and continues to grow in new regions all over the world.

The philosophical teachings of the Buddha were accompanied by an ever-increasing volume of imagery, including sculpted and painted images of the Buddhas, bodhisattvas and deities of the Buddhist pantheon and depictions of the Buddhist cosmos. Temples, monasteries and reliquaries also evolved as locations for the veneration of the Buddha and his teachings, and the wide range of rituals conducted by priests, monks and lay worshippers led to the creation of numerous ritual objects decorated with Buddhist motifs and symbols.

One of the main reasons for the success of this religion is its ability to adapt to the various cultures it encountered and to co-exist in relative harmony with native religions. As Buddhism grew in the different regions of Asia, its teachings evolved to meet the specific needs of the local population, and the development of Buddhist imagery and decoration was strongly affected by local artistic styles and available materials. This has led to the emergence over two millennia of a vast and complex body of Buddhist art of different forms and styles.

The Emergence of Buddhism and Buddhist Art in India

The Story of the Buddha

The story of Buddhism begins in northeastern India and Nepal in the sixth century BC, when Hinduism was the predominant religious and social system in the region (see map, p. 11). In the kingdom of Kapilavastu (now in Nepal), the ruler of the Shakya warrior clan, King Shuddhodana, and his wife, Queen Maya, gave birth to a son, Siddhartha. What we know about the life of Siddhartha is woven together from various Buddhist legends written long after his death. However, some elements in his story are consistent in all the legends.

From the moment he was born, Siddhartha seemed destined for an extraordinary existence. Shortly after his birth, the renowned Indian sage, Ashita, examined the boy and predicted that he would become either a great king or a great spiritual teacher. Determined that his son would become a mighty ruler, the King confined his son to the royal palace, surrounding him with luxury and comfort and preventing him from

The Buddha's hand touching the earth at the moment of enlightenment, stone, Wat Sri Chum, Sukhothai, Thailand

witnessing any misery or pain. Siddhartha lived there until he was about twenty-nine years old. He married a beautiful woman, Yasodhara, and they had a son, Rahula.

However, a spiritual restlessness grew within him. His father had built him four pleasure gardens in close proximity to the palace. One day, on the way to the first three gardens, Siddhartha encountered an old man, weakened and disfigured with age, a second man, sick and on the verge of death, and a funeral procession. These three encounters awakened him to human suffering and instilled in him a determination to seek deliverance from this suffering. On the way to the fourth garden, he met an itinerant monk who was begging for alms. This figure appeared to possess an inner tranquillity that Siddhartha had never before witnessed. Convinced that he too should enter a life of religious and spiritual practice, Siddhartha left his family's palace and embarked upon a new life as the itinerant monk, Gautama.

For six years, Gautama studied and mastered the teachings of various spiritual leaders, and practised strict asceticism, starving himself until he was no more than a skeleton. At this point, however, he realized that enlightenment could not be attained through extreme behaviour, so he began to eat again and rebuild his strength. Once revitalized, he began to sense that his spiritual awakening, or enlightenment, was imminent. He arrived in Bodh Gaya and was drawn to a pipal tree (ficus religiosa). He sat under the tree facing east and meditated here for forty-nine days. On the forty-ninth day, he attained a spiritual awakening, or enlightenment.

This enlightenment, known to Buddhists as nirvana, was essentially a profound understanding of the nature of life and subsequent release from the perpetual cycle of rebirth known as samsara. Hindus, and later Buddhists, believed that one's actions, or karma, determined the level of the soul's rebirth after death. The perpetual nature of this cycle meant that there was no end to the transmigration of the soul, and that rebirth in hell or one of the lower realms of rebirth was always a possibility.

Now an enlightened or awakened being, Gautama became known as the Buddha, or the 'Awakened One'. He was also given the title, Shakyamuni, 'Sage of the Shakya

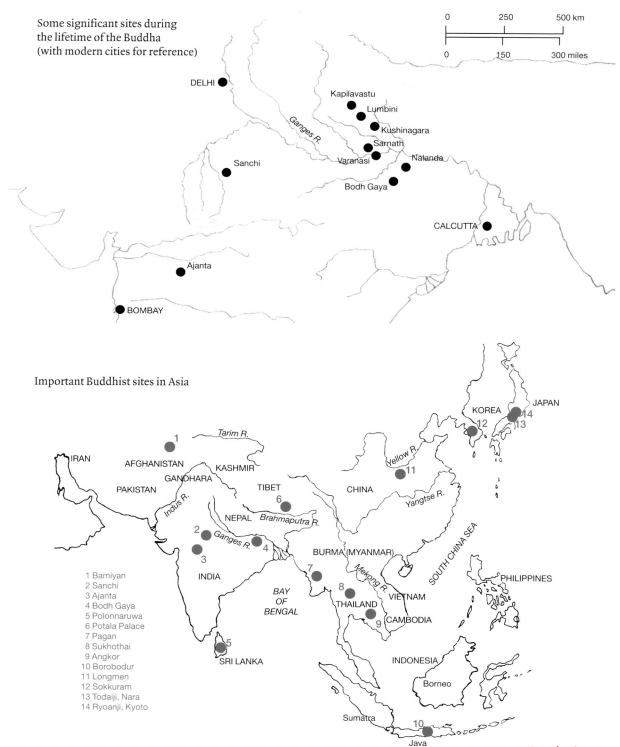

Some significant sites during the lifetime of the Buddha (with modern cities for reference)

0 250 500 km

0 150 300 miles

DELHI

Kapilavastu

Lumbini

Kushinagara

Sarnath

Varanasi

Nalanda

Sanchi

Bodh Gaya

CALCUTTA

Ajanta

BOMBAY

Ganges R.

Important Buddhist sites in Asia

Tarim R.

IRAN

AFGHANISTAN

KASHMIR

GANDHARA

PAKISTAN

TIBET

CHINA

Yellow R.

KOREA

JAPAN

Indus R.

NEPAL

Brahmaputra R.

Ganges R.

BURMA (MYANMAR)

Mekong R.

Yangtse R.

SOUTH CHINA SEA

PHILIPPINES

INDIA

BAY
OF
BENGAL

THAILAND

VIETNAM

CAMBODIA

SRI LANKA

INDONESIA

Borneo

Sumatra

Java

1 Bamiyan
2 Sanchi
3 Ajanta
4 Bodh Gaya
5 Polonnaruwa
6 Potala Palace
7 Pagan
8 Sukhothai
9 Angkor
10 Borobodur
11 Longmen
12 Sokkuram
13 Todaiji, Nara
14 Ryoanji, Kyoto

clan'. He called his philosophy the Middle Way, since he discouraged extreme behaviour such as the pursuit of strict asceticism or excessive luxury, in favour of moderation in all aspects of life. His teachings emphasized compassion towards all beings as a means of cultivating inner peace and progressing towards spiritual release. Shakyamuni summarized his understanding of life in the Four Noble Truths: (1) In all life, there is suffering; (2) Suffering is caused by desire or attachment; (3) To end suffering, one must transcend desire and attachment; (4) To transcend desire and attachment, one must follow the Eightfold Path. The Eightfold Path consists of: Right View, Right Resolve, Right Speech, Right Action, Right Livelihood, Right Effort, Right Mindfulness, and Right Concentration.

The Buddha travelled all over India teaching his philosophy, or dharma ('Law'), to commoners and kings alike and attracted many disciples and followers. He died at the age of eighty or eighty-one in a grove of sala trees in Kushinagara in northern India and thus attained parinirvana, or final release.

The Early Development of the Buddhist Faith

The Buddha did not write down any of his teachings. Over the next few centuries, high-ranking monks, major disciples and enlightened arhats, or Buddhist holy men, who headed the many groups of Buddhist followers all over India, held Councils to preserve the teachings of the Master and to codify the rules of the monastic order (sangha). The Buddha's teachings were defined and spread by missionaries throughout India, Sri Lanka, and areas of Southeast Asia. It was only around the first century AD that the essence of the doctrine was transcribed in Buddhist texts, or sutras.

A major figure in the spread of Buddhism throughout the Indian subcontinent was King Ashoka (ruled c. 272–31 BC). Ashoka ruled the Mauryan Empire at the time of the Third Buddhist Council in around 250 BC, which was held to deal with the rifts that were beginning to develop within the Buddhist community. Determined to disseminate the Buddha's teachings, Ashoka sent missionaries all over the empire, erected pillars with lion capitals and bearing edicts promoting Buddhism, and stupas containing holy Buddhist relics at major Buddhist pilgrimage sites. Ashoka became the model for many Buddhist rulers in Central and East Asia who united their empires under the Buddhist Law. He was the first royal patron of Buddhist art.

Around the first century AD, a schism at one of the Buddhist Councils resulted in the emergence of Mahayana, or 'Greater Vehicle', Buddhism, which distinguished itself from the Hinayana, or 'Lesser Vehicle', a term that Mahayanists apply to the earlier monastic tradition, in which monks follow the teachings of the Buddha as a means of attaining personal enlightenment or salvation. Mahayana Buddhism, which arose in part to meet the spiritual needs of growing numbers of lay Buddhists, teaches that the pursuit of enlightenment can be assisted by bodhisattvas, compassionate beings who postpone their own imminent enlightenment in order to help others attain salvation. It also teaches that more than one Buddha, including the Five transcendental Dhyani Buddhas, can exist in space and time, so has a considerably more elaborate cosmology and pantheon. The Mahayana pantheon gradually grew to encompass not only Buddhas and bodhisattvas, but also numerous deities, often borrowed from the Hindu pantheon, as well as guardian figures who acted as protectors of the Buddhist Law.

Slightly later, in first half of the first millennium, a third tradition, Vajrayana, or 'Diamond/Thunderbolt Vehicle' Buddhism, emerged in India out of the tradition of Tantrism, which is also an aspect of the Hindu and Jain religions. This form of Buddhism emphasizes the compassionate bodhisattvas and numerous other deities who can help practitioners towards salvation. Also known as esoteric or tantric Buddhism, this tradition uses the tantras, or ancient Indian magical texts, as well as elaborate imagery, rituals, hand gestures, sound and visualization devices as means to attain spiritual perfection or enlightenment.

Both the traditional monastic schools, including Theravada, 'the School of the Elders', and the Mahayana tradition flourished in India until around the sixth century, when Hinduism and later Islam became more dominant. By the twelfth century, Buddhism had all but disappeared from India. However, before this time, Theravada Buddhism had spread to Sri Lanka and areas of Southeast Asia, and is often known as the Southern Tradition of Buddhism. Meanwhile, Mahayana Buddhism had spread to China, Korea, and Japan, and around the seventh and eighth centuries, Vajrayana Buddhism took hold in Tibet, Nepal and Mongolia and travelled as far as China and Japan. The Mahayana and Vajrayana schools are together often referred to as the Northern Traditions of Buddhism.

The Development of Buddhist Imagery in India

For the first few centuries following the death of the Buddha, no Buddhist art or literature was produced, and figural depictions of the Buddha did not appear until around the first century BC. Before this time, Buddhist art was primarily an-iconic, featuring numerous symbols that represented the Buddha's teachings, rather than iconic figures depicting him in human form. The earliest Buddhist art appeared around the third century BC around the time of Ashoka, on the famous pillars that he erected at sites of Buddhist pilgrimages. These pillars were beautifully carved with details that are rich in Buddhist symbolism. At the top of the columns are three lions, regal beasts which are believed to roar out the Buddha's teachings throughout the world. They are seated on lotuses, which symbolize purity, and they originally supported a great wheel, or chakra, which symbolizes the wheel of the Buddhist law that was set into motion at the Buddha's first sermon at Sarnath.

Ashoka also erected 84,000 stupas, burial mounds that contained relics of the Buddha. Stupas were some of the most important symbols of the Buddhist faith, representing at once the Buddha's teachings and his final enlightenment. Surrounding many large stupas, including the famous examples at Sanchi, India, were stone gates carved with scenes from the life of the Buddha, as well as an-iconic motifs such as sacred trees, small images of stupas, and giant wheels seated on

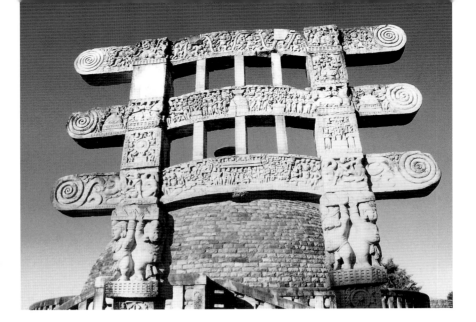

The carved stone gate at the Great Stupa at Sanchi, India, first century AD

thrones, representing the teachings of the Buddha. In many other early Buddhist stone carvings, most notably the relief carvings of Amaravati in southern India, an empty throne is used to imply the presence of the Buddha, as are images of a riderless horse with an umbrella held over it, or a pair of footprints. The Buddha himself is not represented, apparently implying his non-presence, or transcendence of this world.

There is much debate over where and when the first human images of the Buddha appeared. One of the first datable images of the Buddha as a human figure is on a gold coin dating to the first century AD, during the reign of the Kushan ruler, King Kanishka. The extensive Kushan empire had two capitals, one in Gandhara (in modern Pakistan, Afghanistan and northwestern India), the other in Mathura in north-central India. It was in these two centres that the first images of the Buddha and bodhisattvas began to appear around the first century AD, in response to the growth of devotionalism in India's major religious traditions, and more specifically in response to the emergence of Mahayana Buddhism, in which the bodhisattva saviour figure plays a major role. In Gandhara, images of Buddhas and bodhisattvas with European facial features, wavy hair and moustaches, and wearing toga-like robes show the strong influence of Greco-Roman artistic styles. In Mathura, however, a more Indian style of figures evolved, wearing Indian clothing and with rounder, often smiling, facial features.

Indian Buddhist art is believed by many to have reached its Golden Age during the Gupta period (fourth and fifth centuries AD), when graceful stone figures of the Buddha and bodhisattvas were carved in a truly Indian style. This style eventually travelled beyond India's borders and influenced the Buddhist art of other regions. The murals painted in the caves of Ajanta, created in the fifth and sixth centuries, are some of the earliest and finest examples of a tradition of Buddhist cave paintings that spread throughout Asia.

After the Gupta period, Buddhism began a slow, steady decline in India, although it was gaining momentum in many other regions. The Pala kingdom, in particular, in what is now Bengal and Bihar in northeastern India, continued the Buddhist artistic tradition for a few more centuries, creating many fine works in a more elaborate style that was transmitted to areas of Southeast Asia. By the end of the twelfth century, Buddhism had almost disappeared in the Indian subcontinent, although many masterpieces of art, including temples, stupas, cave paintings, and sculptures, have remained from the earlier periods.

The Spread of Buddhism and its Arts

Sri Lanka

Sri Lanka has been a centre of Buddhism for over two thousand years. According to one legend, the Buddha visited the island on three separate occasions, and it is believed that two hundred years later, King Ashoka's son, Mahinda, brought a branch of the original bodhi tree from Bodh Gaya to Sri Lanka and planted it at the first capital, Anuradhapura, where a descendant of this tree is still worshipped today. Mahinda also converted the Sri Lankan King Devanampiya-Tissa (c. 250–210 BC) to Buddhism, and from that period onward, Buddhism in various forms was practised on the island. The first Buddhist texts, or sutras, were written in Pali, the language of Sri Lanka. By the eleventh century, the monastic Theravada school gained primacy and thrived under the Sinhalese rulers of Sri Lanka. In the twelfth and thirteenth centuries, a period when India was rejecting the Buddhist faith in favour of Hinduism and Islam, Sri Lanka became an important Buddhist centre, spreading Theravada teachings from the monasteries of the capital, Polonnaruwa, into areas of Southeast Asia, including Thailand and Burma.

In Sri Lanka, the principal object of devotion is the bodhi tree at Anuradhapura, as it represents the place of the Buddha's enlightenment. It has been surrounded by a shrine and four seated Buddhas. The stupa, a symbol of the Buddha's enlightenment, features prominently in Sri Lankan Buddhist architecture, the most important example also being at Anuradhapura. Unlike many of the stupas from India and other Buddhist cultures, the Sri Lankan stupas feature minimal decoration, the form itself being of greater importance than decorative details.

In Theravada Buddhist cultures such as Sri Lanka, the principal figure of veneration is the Historical Buddha, so the art of these cultures generally focuses on Shakyamuni and the various important events of his historical life. Jataka tales, or tales of his previous lives as a bodhisattva, also feature prominently in the art of these cultures. The most outstanding examples of Sri Lankan Buddhist sculptures are the colossal stone images of the Buddha and other figures at the Gal Vihara temple at Polonnaruwa (see p. 182). These figures and many other Sri Lankan images from the twelfth and thirteenth centuries show the stylistic influence of the graceful sculptures of the earlier Indian Gupta period. After the thirteenth century, Sri Lanka experienced an increasing fusion of religions, with shrines combining Buddhist and Hindu worship, and Mahayana figures such the compassionate bodhisattva Avalokiteshvara gaining a devout following.

Southeast Asia

Buddhism was introduced to Southeast Asia in the second or third centuries AD However, due to the popularity of Hinduism, which was transmitted to this region from India at an earlier date, Buddhism only became a powerful force here in the sixth and seventh century. Although both the Mahayana and Vajrayana schools of Buddhism did have a presence in Southeast Asia for a short period, especially on the islands of Java and Sumatra, the dominant Buddhist tradition in this region is Theravada Buddhism, which came to these regions from southeast India and Sri Lanka. The earliest Buddhist art from Southeast Asia tends to be highly derivative of the Indian models that were brought by proselytising monks. However, by the end of the first millennium, the different Buddhist regions of Southeast Asia had begun to produce their own unique styles and art forms patronized by their various rulers.

Thailand

Seated Buddha at Sukhothai, brick and stucco, thirteenth or fourteenth century, Thailand

In the area now known as Thailand, Buddhism was first adopted at an official level by the Mon people, who ruled over central Thailand from the sixth to the eleventh centuries AD. This Buddhist state has become known as Dvaravati, and many examples of Theravada and Mahayana sculptures in stone, bronze and terracotta have survived from this period. These figures, usually depicting the Buddha's enlightenment and other key moments in his life, may be the earliest Buddhist sculptures made in Southeast Asia. Artists of this period also created many images of the Buddhist wheel of the Law, either on its own or flanked by deer, symbolizing the Buddha's first sermon at the Deer Park at Sarnath, a moment which marked the true beginning of Buddhism as a faith. Large numbers of stupas, made from brick and laterite (a clay-like material), were also built during this period and decorated with niches containing terracotta clay figures. Later, this area came under the influence of the Khmer kingdoms of Cambodia who invaded the area, and until the thirteenth century, much of Thai Buddhist art echoes Khmer examples.

In the thirteenth century, the Thai people, who originally came from China, established the kingdom of Sukhothai in north central Thailand, which lasted until 1438. This Buddhist kingdom had close links with the Theravada centres in Sri Lanka, and much of the Buddhist architecture of the period reveals influences from Sri Lanka, as well as the Khmer and Mon cultures. Sukhothai period figures of the Buddha are characterized by their graceful physiques, gentle, yet elegant faces and a flame-shaped ushnisha, or protrusion, on the top of the head. The most notable development in Sukhothai Buddhist imagery is the walking Buddha, a graceful figure with a curvaceous form, one leg extended in front of the other.

From 1350 in lower Thailand, another Buddhist kingdom was established at Ayudhaya and lasted until it was sacked by the Burmese in 1767. The Buddhist art and architecture of this period shows much Khmer and Mon stylistic influence. This is most apparent at Ayudhaya, where Khmer-style towers, or prang, gently curved structures ending in a point, are found alongside traditional Thai-style stupas with their attenuated forms and lotus bud finials. After the demise of Ayudhaya, Buddhism has continued to flourish in Thailand, as have its arts, which in the past two centuries have been characterized by elaborate surface decoration, often including gilding, coloured glass and gems, and wall paintings.

Cambodia

The area that is now Cambodia was ruled by the Khmer from as early as the sixth century. The Khmer kings followed both Hinduism and Buddhism, and under their rule, fine stone sculptures and temples were created, at first copying Indian models, but increasingly in Khmer style. Khmer royal patronage of Buddhism increased over the next few centuries and reached its culmination under one of the most powerful and influential of all the Khmer rulers, Jayavarman VII (ruled 1181–1219).

Under his reign, some of Cambodia's most remarkable Buddhist architecture was built, in particular the Bayon, a Buddhist monument in the Angkor Thom complex. This is an architectural manifestation of Jayavarman's Mahayanist Buddhist beliefs and a demonstration of his belief in the concept of the god-king, a divine ruler at the centre of the universe. The Bayon is designed as a great cosmic mountain, symbolizing the Buddhist Mount Meru at the centre of the cosmos and is built on a base that resembles a Buddhist mandala, or cosmic diagram. On its towers are numerous faces of the bodhisattva Avalokiteshvara looking out to the four directions. The faces are said to resemble his own looking out over his great empire.

Images of Avalokiteshvara were produced in large numbers under Jayavarman, mostly in stone, but occasionally in bronze. Khmer sculptors also created numerous images of the Historical Buddha, often shown surrounded by the hood of the seven-headed serpent king, Muchalinda, who protected the Buddha from a storm during his meditation under the bodhi tree. This image, as well as sculpted and painted images of naga, or serpent deities, were extremely popular in Khmer Buddhist art, in part because Jayavarman VII also associated himself with the Buddha, who was protected by snakes. After his rule, patronage of Buddhism and its arts declined in Cambodia, and the era of great Khmer Buddhist art came to an end.

Burma (Myanmar)

The earliest evidence of Buddhism in Burma dates to the fifth century AD, when the country was settled largely by the Mon people who inhabited both Burma and Thailand. The Mon had their political and cultural centre in the Dvaravati state in what is now central Thailand, but the Mon people in the area of Burma had their capital at Thaton, and are known to have had contacts with India and Buddhism. The first major

Shwedagon Pagoda at night, Rangoon (Yangon), Burma (Myanmar), rebuilt eighteenth century

Buddhist capital was Sri Ksetra, a Pyu city, which, according to the seventh-century Chinese pilgrim Xuanzang, had one hundred elaborately decorated Buddhist monasteries. This and other Pyu sites have revealed that the Pyu people, who entered Burma from the northeast, believed in a mixture of Hinduism and Mahayana and Theravada Buddhism. Regrettably, little Buddhist art has survived from this early period.

The oldest Buddhist archaeological remains and the first appearance of a true Burmese style in Buddhist art date to the time of King Aniruddha (ruled 1044–77), whose enthronement united Burma for the first time and began the Pagan period (1044–1287). King Aniruddha is known to have been an ardent Buddhist who spread the Buddha's teachings to the areas he conquered. He brought monks, artists, and craftsmen from conquered Buddhist cities to the capital, Pagan, to develop it into a truly Buddhist city. In the three hundred or so years that Pagan was the capital, several thousand temples were constructed in the city, of which about two thousand remain. Most of these were Theravada Buddhist temples, although this religion co-existed alongside Mahayana Buddhism and Hinduism until around the thirteenth century, when Theravada gained primacy.

The city of Pagan is remarkable for its extraordinary scale and for the impressive brick and stucco Buddhist architecture that is unique in Southeast Asia. Many of the temples, including the Ananda temple built around 1105, resemble stupas, with their stepped pyramid bases, bell-like central sections and spires, all painted white with stucco to create the impression of a stone structure. The stupas, or pagodas, of Pagan and other Burmese cities also have a distinctly Burmese flavour. The Shwezigon Pagoda of Pagan and the later Shwedagon Pagoda of Rangoon (Yangon) stretch upwards, their separate geometric parts merging into a single golden form with smooth profile (see above).

In sculpture, images of the Historical Buddha are the most common, either standing or seated with his right hand in the earth-touching gesture, signifying the Buddha's enlightenment (see below left). In many images, the Buddha is depicted

Seated Buddha touching the earth, lacquered wood, Burma (Myanmar), c. 1200.

wearing a crown, a reference to a legend in which the Buddha takes on the appearance of a powerful monarch in order to win the respect and faith of a certain Indian king. In later images of the Buddha, the Buddha is often shown standing wearing flowing robes and covered in jewels.

Indonesia

The islands of Java and Sumatra in Indonesia enjoyed active trade with the mainland of India from around the sixth or seventh century, resulting in the introduction of both Hinduism and Buddhism to the islands. In the eighth century, Mahayana and Buddhist teachings were transmitted to the islands from the Pala empire in northeastern India. This accounts in part for the creation there of Borobodur, one of the most complex and mysterious works of architecture and sculpture in the Buddhist world.

Built by rulers of the Shailendra kingdom (730–930), Borobodur is unlike many Buddhist structures in Southeast Asia. The structure is neither a temple that was entered by worshippers, nor a stupa that was circumambulated. In fact, the stupa does not have prominent position in the temples of Java. Instead, Borobodur, which was built around 800 AD, closely resembles a three-dimensional mandala, or cosmic diagram of a perfected world, from the Vajrayana Buddhist tradition. It does feature images of the life of the Buddha and Jataka tales, and some 70 small stupas, all of which are important in the Theravada tradition (see p. 190). However, the structure represents the syncretic nature of Javanese religious beliefs, which blend Theravada and Mahayana elements. These two Buddhist traditions lost their importance two hundred years later after the demise of the Shailendra kingdom in Java. The island then became predominantly Hindu until the end of the fifteenth century, when Islam ended Buddhist and Hindu activity.

Central Asia

It was roughly three hundred years after the death of the Historical Buddha before Buddhism began to spread outside India. In the third century BC, during the reign of King Ashoka, the teachings of the Buddha spread south to the island of Sri Lanka. Missionaries also travelled to Gandhara in present-day northwestern India, Pakistan and east Afghanistan, where Buddhism took hold fairly quickly. The region of Gandhara was situated along a branch of the Silk Road, along which silks and other merchandise were transported between China and the West. Buddhism also spread along this route, carried by Buddhist monks and pilgrims who settled in the various regions connected by the route, built Buddhist temples and monasteries, and proselytised among the local communities. Over the centuries, many cave temples and Buddhist monuments were erected along the route at Bamiyan and Gilgit, and then further east at Kucha and Dunhuang towards the Chinese end of the Silk Road. Many of these Buddhist sites flourished in the first centuries AD, and they contain some of the earliest surviving Buddhist texts and imagery.

China

Buddhism first travelled towards China along the Silk Road, penetrating its borders during the first century AD. Initially, the religion encountered resistance from followers of the two native philosophies, Confucianism and Daoism. However, Indian monks gradually adapted Buddhism to suit the beliefs of the Chinese, and eventually, many of the scholarly Confucian Chinese embraced the monastic traditions of Buddhism, while the more intuitive and non-ritualistic Daoists embraced Mahayana teachings. Under the Turkic Wei rulers between the fourth and the sixth century, Buddhism flourished, and huge Buddhist cave temples at Yungang and Longmen were created as displays of Wei support of the faith. At Dunhuang, at the Chinese entrance to the Silk Road, many more cave temples were decorated with Buddhist sculptures and paintings and the site went on to be a major Buddhist centre for pilgrims until the end of the first millennium.

Some of the most remarkable works of Chinese Buddhist art date from this early period. Sculptural representations of all sizes of the Buddha and bodhisattvas, often with Chinese facial features, were among the greatest achievements of this early period. The large stone figures carved from cliffs and the small stone and bronze figures with their sweet-smiling faces and heavily stylized robes became the model for Buddhist imagery throughout East Asia. It was also during this time that the pagoda, an East Asian variation of the stupa, made its appearance in China. Pagodas retain the solid core which houses the relics and a space around them for circumambulation, but these tower-like structures with their many storeys bear little resemblance to their Indian ancestors.

During the first half of the Tang dynasty (618–908), Buddhism received the support of many of the Chinese rulers, who were drawn to the Indian concept of the *chakravartin*, or Buddhist king who ruled over all other kings. They erected many large stone sculptures of Buddhas, and patronized temples and monasteries, resulting in a blossoming of Chinese Buddhist culture. Very few of these buildings have survived, but examples of Tang-style Chinese architecture in Japan attest to the sophistication and elegance of these Tang Buddhist temples. During this period, many different schools of Buddhism achieved great popularity, from the complex, ritualistic esoteric schools to the meditative Chan school, which drew many elements from Daoism. Two major Chinese Buddhist schools that blossomed at this time were the Pure Land school, which stressed the saving powers of the Buddha Amitabha, and the Tiantai school, named after a sacred mountain in southern China, which preached the potential for Buddhahood in all beings. The imagery created for these various schools is among the most refined Buddhist imagery ever created. The few Tang dynasty paintings that have survived from Dunhuang and the stone and bronze sculptures reveal a graceful, dynamic artistic style reminiscent of the elegant Gupta style of India.

In the later Tang dynasty, Buddhists were heavily persecuted, but over the following centuries, Buddhism received sporadic support from Chinese emperors of the Song (960–1279) and later the Ming (1368–1644) and Qing (1644–1911) dynasties, who commissioned imagery of various forms and styles. The compassionate bodhisattva Avalokiteshvara, known in Chinese as Guanyin, became one of the most popular objects of veneration, and underwent a transformation into a merciful goddess. Close contact between the Chinese court and Tibetan lamas during the Ming dynasty resulted in the Tibetan influence on Chinese Buddhist art at several points in time, and the introduction of Chinese artistic elements and motifs into Tibetan Buddhist art.

Korea

From China, Buddhism was transmitted to Korea and Japan, where it has endured to varying degrees up to the present day. Buddhism first appeared on the Korean peninsula during the fourth century, when the area was divided into three main kingdoms: Koguryo, Paekche and Silla. Before the introduction of Buddhism, the Koreans, many of whom were descended from nomadic peoples from the Siberia-Manchuria region, were a shamanistic people, believing strongly in the world of spirits. Buddhism arrived first in the northern kingdom of Koguryo, via an overland route from northeast China, and shortly afterwards in Paekche, via the sea from southern China. The kingdom of Silla in the southeast was relatively isolated and received Buddhism later than the other two states, although the faith eventually took the strongest hold in this region.

Avalokiteshvara seated in royal ease position, wood, China, twelfth or thirteenth century

Buddhist imagery from this period bore a strong resemblance to early Chinese Buddhist images from the fifth and sixth centuries. The sculptures of this period feature simple forms and shallow, tentative carving. Buddha images tend to have large heads and hands, similar to the earlier Chinese figures at Longmen, and the folds of their robes are highly stylized. Their faces wear gentle smiles. Some of the most notable figures of this period are the bronze seated figures of Maitreya, the Buddha of the Future, from Paekche and Silla, depicted as a bodhisattva sitting in contemplation of the state of the world. Dating to the seventh century, these images show the beginnings of a true Korean sculptural style of slender, elegant Buddhist figures.

When the three kingdoms were united by the Silla in 668 AD, Buddhism thrived in the southeast under the influence of neighbouring Tang dynasty China. In the capital, Kyongju, numerous temples, monasteries, and pagodas were built by the rulers and members of the upper classes. One of the most notable sites is the Pulguksa, the Temple of the Buddha Land, constructed by Prime Minister Kim Taesong in the eighth century (see p. 22). This large complex, which has since been destroyed and rebuilt, features Chinese Tang-style wooden architecture as well as stone pagodas that demonstrate a native Korean architectural style, with open sections and steps on each side. The Sokkuram Cave Temple was also created at this time by Kim Taesong as a temple of private worship. Inside it is Korea's great masterpiece of Buddhist art, a granite statue of a seated Buddha, probably Shakyamuni, surrounded on the walls by relief carvings of bodhisattvas and monks. The cave was a more intimate version of the Indian, Central Asian and Chinese Buddhist cave temples and featured openings which allowed the sunlight to stream in and animate the carvings on the wall.

Entrance to Pulguksa temple, Kyongju, Korea, originally built in the eighth century, rebuilt in the twentieth century

Buddhism continued to flourish in Korea during the succeeding Koryo dynasty (918–1391), when many fine Buddhist paintings on silk were produced for the Buddhist nobility. Other significant artistic achievements of this period include bronze temple bells, lacquer sutra boxes, and ceramic sprinkling vessels, all used by Buddhist monks and lay practitioners. One of the most spectacular achievements of Korean Buddhists was the carving of the entire Buddhist canon, or Tripitaka, onto woodblocks to enable the printing and widespread dissemination of Buddhist teachings. A set of 81,137 woodblocks carved in the thirteenth century is still housed in a special hall in the Heinsa temple. After this period, Buddhism lost the patronage of the rulers, who turned to Confucianism for philosophical guidance. However, many of the ordinary people still practised Buddhism and produced folk art with Buddhist subject matter.

The pagoda at the Horyuji temple, Nara, Japan, late seventh or early eighth century

Japan

It was the Koreans who first introduced Buddhism to Japan. According to Japanese historical records, the King of Paekche sent Buddhist texts, a bronze image and other religious objects to the Japanese Emperor Kimmu in the sixth century. Initially, Japan's imperial court, who derived much of their political power from the belief that they were descended from the chief Shinto deity, the Sun Goddess, were wary of introducing a foreign faith that might undermine their position. However, an imperial prince, Shotoku Taishi (574–794), encouraged the study and spread of Buddhism among the country's rulers, and commissioned the country's first temples, paintings, and sculptures.

The earliest Japanese Buddhist art and architecture of the seventh century strongly echoes that of China and Korea of a slightly earlier date. Temples around the ancient capital of Nara housed bronze and wooden Buddhas and bodhisattvas, created mostly for the personal worship of the ruling classes. In the eighth century, the devout Buddhist Emperor Shomu transformed the nation into a Buddhist state with himself as a chakravartin, in the centre. To demonstrate his own greatness as well as to encourage the spread of the faith, he constructed a colossal bronze image of the Cosmic Buddha Vairochana in the capital, Nara, and installed it in the largest wooden structure ever created.

After Shomu, church and state separated again in Japan, and Buddhism became more of a personal faith. Throughout the ninth and tenth centuries, many different schools of the Mahayana tradition took hold in Japan, including the esoteric Tendai and Shingon sects and the Pure Land sect. The Buddha Amitabha and the bodhisattva Avalokiteshvara become the focus of devotional Buddhism, first among the upper classes and then increasingly among the general populace. Some of Japan's greatest contributions to Buddhist art are the wooden sculptural representations of these and other Buddhist figures, from the serene gilded wood image of the Buddha Amitabha at the Byodoin temple near Kyoto, to the dynamic wood guardian figures at the temple gates of Nara and Kyoto temples such as the Todaiji. Also masterfully created are the wooden worship halls and pagodas of Japan's Buddhist temples, some of which have survived since the eighth century (see below left).

Zen gravel garden at Ginkakuji temple, Kyoto

Around the twelfth century, Zen Buddhism, which evolved from Chinese Chan meditational practices, gained a following among the samurai military class and later in other areas of society. Within the context of Zen Buddhism, Buddhist paintings and calligraphy, often based on Chinese Chan Buddhist prototypes, flourished, and the dry landscape gardens of Zen temples became some of the most exquisite sites for Buddhist meditational practices (see right). From around the seventeenth century, Buddhism lost the patronage of the rulers and became more of a people's religion.

Nepal

Siddhartha Gautama, the Historical Buddha, was born at Lumbini in the Shakyan capital of Kapilavastu in the southern region of Nepal. However, after he left home to pursue spiritual enlightenment, Siddhartha spent most of the next fifty years of his life travelling around India. It is said that King Ashoka visited Nepal in the third century BC, bringing with him the Buddhist faith and erecting a stupa and one of his famous columns at Lumbini. Buddhism was practised alongside Hinduism in Nepal for several centuries, and it enjoyed its greatest popularity between the eighth and the thirteenth centuries. From the thirteenth century onwards, Hinduism has been the predominant faith of Nepal.

Nepal fully embraced the esoteric teachings of Vajrayana Buddhism, along with its numerous forms of the Buddha and its various benign and wrathful bodhisattvas and deities. Along with images of the Historical Buddha at various stages of his life, and bodhisattvas, particularly Avalokiteshvara and the female figures, Tara and Prajnaparamita feature prominently in Nepali imagery. Probably the most remarkable examples of Nepali Buddhist art are the fine gilt bronze sculptures produced by the Newari metalworkers of the Kathmandu Valley. These bronze figures are slender, graceful deities usually wearing crowns and jewelry made using inlaid precious stones. Stupas and other objects of veneration were given the same artistic treatment by the metalworkers of Nepal.

In the realm of painting, the most notable works are mandalas, often similar to Tibetan examples, and palm leaf manuscripts decorated with gold lettering and bold colours. In architecture, the most remarkable developments in Nepal were probably their Buddhist buildings constructed out of brick and wood. Many of the temple buildings have wide wooden eaves that extend outwards to resemble those of East Asian pagodas. As well as temple buildings, the Nepali Buddhists constructed large and small stupas, close in style to the Indian prototypes, with a large dome surmounted by a rectangular element called a harmika and a spire with umbrella. A unique feature of Nepali stupas is the addition of a pair of eyes painted on each side of the harmika, which may serve as the eyes of the Four Heavenly Kings who guard the four directions of the world, or as the eyes of the all-seeing Cosmic Buddha, Vairochana.

Tibet

Buddhism did not arrive in Tibet until the seventh century AD, a relatively late date compared with the rest of Asia, and it took another three hundred years for it to become firmly rooted. It was Vajrayana Buddhism that found favour among the Tibetans, who possessed a strong tradition of shamanistic practices which they incorporated into their form of Buddhism. Often known as Lamaism, after the Tibetan name for a Buddhist monk, Tibetan Buddhism is often considered the most complex of all Buddhist traditions. Not only are many different Buddhas, bodhisattvas, and deities venerated, but they are worshipped in a great number of different forms. Of great importance to Tibetan Buddhists is the concept of mystical union with deities which can be achieved by performing mantras (sacred phrases), *mudras* (hand gestures) and meditation using a variety of different types of art forms, the most well known being the elaborate diagrams known as mandalas.

The Buddhist art of Tibet evolved under the influences of Indian, Nepalese, Kashmiri and Chinese artistic styles. In the realm of sculpture, stone carving is virtually unknown in Tibet, but many bronze figures of bodhisattvas and deities have been made, often by the Newari craftsmen of Nepal and their descendants. These share with the Nepalese images an elaborate, heavily ornamented style. Some of the most remarkable sculptural images are the figures of male and female deities joined in sexual embrace. Known as yab-yum, or 'father-mother' images, these figures symbolize the union of wisdom (female) and compassion (male) that is believed by many Mahayana Buddhists to be necessary for enlightenment. The most striking of these figures are the wrathful deities, with their bulging eyes, fangs and many arms wielding swords with which they destroy evil. Other notable Tibetan images are the figures of the various deified teachers, or gurus, of Tibetan Buddhism, including Padmasambhava, who brought many Tantric practices to Tibet in the eighth century, and Atisha, who helped reform Buddhism in the eleventh century.

Buddhist painting has flourished in Tibet, and paintings on cloth, known as thangkas, are particularly remarkable (see opposite title page). They generally depict a Buddha, bodhisattva, deity or deified guru in the centre, surrounded by lesser deities. They may be shown in their various paradises, or pure lands, or in the centre of a mandala, a geometrical diagram that represents the perfected worlds of these deities. Originally derived from Indian Tantric diagrams, these mandalas have been used by Tibetan Buddhists in visualization exercizes that help the practitioner to enter the perfected worlds and progress towards enlightenment (see p. 174).

For centuries, Tibet has been one of the most devoutly Buddhist countries, and has been one of the few nations in which the political leader has also been the country's religious leader. Over the centuries, this phenomenon resulted in the enthusiastic patronage of Buddhist painting, sculpture and metalwork, in particular. Since 1959, His Holiness, the Dalai Lama, has lived in exile in Dharamasala in India, and many exiled Tibetan Buddhists have established their homes in countries around the world. Many have taken with them the Buddhist arts of Tibet, and increasingly, Tibetan Buddhist thangka paintings, silk appliqués and mandalas are being produced in as distant places as Europe and the United States, where Buddhism is enjoying increasing popularity in the twenty-first century.

1 Shakyamuni gesturing fearlessness, brass, Gandhara, 5th–6th century (left)

2 Shakyamuni leaving his father's palace, Burma, 19th century (above)

3 Shakyamuni as an infant, China, 17th century (below)

Identity

Shakyamuni, 'Sage of the Shakyas', founder of Buddhism, is often referred to simply as the Buddha or the Historical Buddha, although many Buddhists believe that more than one Buddha, or 'enlightened one', has existed in this world. Born in Lumbini (in modern Nepal) in the sixth century BC as Prince Siddhartha Gautama of the Shakya clan, he rejected his royal lifestyle in order to pursue a true understanding of the nature of life. He followed several spiritual leaders, some of whom practised harsh austerities including starvation, but was unsatisfied by their teachings. After years of searching, he achieved spiritual enlightenment, nirvana, after meditating intensely under a pipal tree. From then on, he became known as Shakyamuni or the Buddha.

The Buddha then travelled around India sharing his knowledge until his death, and final enlightenment, or parinirvana, at the age of about eighty. His teachings, or dharma, also known as the Middle Way, emphasize a life of moderation based on the Four Noble Truths: (1) life is full of suffering; (2) the source of suffering is desire or attachment; (3) to end suffering, we must transcend desire and attachment; (4) to do so, we must follow the Eightfold Path of right speech, right livelihood, right action, right effort, right mindfulness, right concentration, right opinion and right intention.

Principal Areas of Worship

Shakyamuni is regarded by most Buddhists not so much as a deity as a perfect holy man who discovered the truth about human suffering and shared his knowledge with others. He is venerated by almost all Buddhists. Whereas the Northern Buddhist traditions of Mahayana and Vajrayana have revered many other Buddhas, bodhisattvas and deities, Shakyamuni is the principal, and often only, figure of worship of the Southern Buddhism of Sri Lanka and Southeast Asia.

Representations and Attributes

For the first six hundred or so years after his death, the Buddha and his teachings were represented in art by images of the wheel (of the law) (47), footprints (46), empty thrones (36), and other symbols of his teachings or his holy presence. Around the first century AD, images of the Buddha began to appear in northern India, depicting the Buddha wearing monk's robes and a serene facial expression. His hands sometimes cradle a monk's begging bowl (60). He is often shown standing or seated in the lotus position, one hand usually gesturing fearlessness (41) (**ill. 1**).

Many images of the Historical Buddha refer to five key moments in his life: his birth; his departure from home; his attainment of enlightenment; his first sermon; his death. These are represented in the Buddhist imagery of most Buddhist cultures.

As an Infant

According to legend, Prince Siddhartha was an extraordinary child and was born with the ability to walk and speak. Immediately after he was born from out of the right side of his mother, Queen Maya, the infant Siddhartha took seven steps in each cardinal

Shijia muni
(Chinese)
Shakamuni
(Japanese)
Sokka muni
(Korean)
Sha-kya thub-pa
(Tibetan)
Sigemuni
(Mongolian)
Thich Ca Mau Ni
Phat *(Vietnamese)*
Phra Phurtha
Chao *(Thai)*

4 Shakyamuni at the moment of enlightenment, gilded bronze, Doi Suthep, Chiang Mai, Thailand (left)

5 The Buddha preaching at the Deer Park in Sarnath, China (right)

6 Shakyamuni at the moment of death, Wat Mongkhon Bophit, Ayudhaya, Thailand (below)

direction and proclaimed, 'I am the only Venerable One in all of Heaven and Earth.' There are many East Asian sculptures depicting this moment. They show the Buddha as an infant standing with one arm pointing upwards to heaven, the other downwards to earth, as if to stake his claim on the universe (**ill. 3**).

Leaving Home

When Siddhartha was about thirty years old, he realized that he wanted to learn the truth about life, human suffering and how to prevent it. He knew that he would not be able to learn what he wanted to know in the confines of his family's palace, so he left his home, wife and child in the middle of the night and embarked on a quest for spiritual enlightenment. His departure from home is often represented by an image of Siddhartha dressed in his princely robes astride a horse (**ill. 2**). The horse is often shown being carried by the gods to prevent the sounds of his departure from awakening his family.

The Moment of Enlightenment

After years of study and self discipline, he attained a true understanding of the nature of life and became the Buddha, or 'Enlightened One'. This occurred while Siddhartha was seated in deep meditation under a pipal tree (51). According to legend, the evil King Mara, determined to prevent Siddhartha from achieving spiritual enlightenment, sent demonic warriors and beautiful temptresses to distract him from his meditation. Siddhartha was not distracted, and succeeded in attaining spiritual enlightenment. At the moment of enlightenment, he reached down with his right hand and called upon the Earth to witness his virtuous deeds and his resolve (43) (**ill. 4**).

First Sermon at the Deer Park

Shortly after his enlightenment, at the Deer Park in Sarnath, near Benares, the Buddha gave his first sermon on the Four Noble Truths and the Eightfold Path as a means of attaining enlightenment (**ill. 5**). This sermon represented the first turning of the Wheel of the Buddhist Teachings, and marked the birth of Buddhism as a faith. In painting and sculpture, the moment is often represented by showing the Buddha seated with his hands in the gesture of turning the wheel of the Buddhist Law (42, 47).

The Moment of Death, or Parinirvana

The Buddha Shakyamuni died peacefully at the age of eighty or eighty-one in a grove of trees near Kushinagara in northern India. He was accompanied by some of his closest disciples, and in many painted representations of his death scene, bodhisattvas, demons, celestial beings, and animals are shown gathering around him on his death bed. In sculptural representations, the Buddha is usually simply depicted lying in his right side and wearing a peaceful, serene expression, at the point of leaving his physical form and passing into final enlightenment, or parinirvana (**ill. 6**).

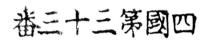

四國第三十三番

1 Seated figure of Bhaishajyaguru, Japan (above)

2 Bhaishajyaguru and attendants, Tibet, 15th century (above right)

3 Bhaishajyaguru Triad, wood-block print, Japan, 20th century (below right)

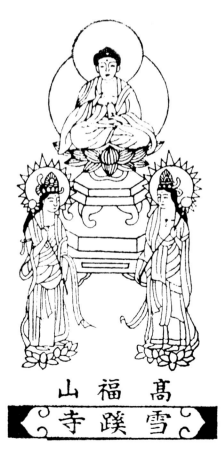

高福山

雪蹊寺

Identity

Bhaishajyaguru, the 'Healing Teacher', is one of the most popular forms of the Buddha and is often known as the Medicine Buddha. While still a bodhisattva, Bhaishajyaguru is said to have made twelve vows, some concerning the healing of the sick. Consequently, as a Buddha, he has the specific task of dispensing spiritual medicine to devotees. He is believed by many to have the power to heal physical ailments also. In some Buddhist texts, Bhaishajyaguru was said to be one of Eight Medicine Buddhas, who created medicinal plants and presided over the seven worlds. In the *Bhaishajyaguru Sutra*, written sometime before the sixth century AD, this Buddha is described as more than a spiritual and physical healer. He is a supreme and cosmic Buddha who illuminates the entire universe.

From Central Asia to Japan, he was believed to command a group of twelve warriors, each representing one of his vows, or the twelve months. These fierce warriors defend the health of the faithful in Bhaishajyaguru's name. Just as Amitabha (6) presides over the Western Paradise, Bhaishajyaguru presides over the Vaidurya-prabhasa, the Lapis Lazuli, or Beryl, Paradise in the East. In certain Chinese Buddhist texts, Bhaishajyaguru is said to welcome those who dream of him at their death into his Paradise.

Principal Areas of Worship

Bhaishajyaguru has not been worshipped widely in India or Southeast Asia. However, he has long been popular in Tibet, China and Japan. In Japan, he was one of the first forms of Buddha to be worshipped and is still popular among Buddhists of various sects, sometimes replacing Akshobhya (5) or Vairochana (4) as one of the five Dhyani Buddhas. He also appears as one of the Thirteen Buddhas of the esoteric Shingon school. These Buddhas are worshipped in a fixed sequence after the death of a loved one; Bhaishajyaguru is believed to look after the soul in the seventh week after death.

Representations and Attributes

Bhaishajyaguru, like Shakyamuni (1), is usually shown as a seated Buddha wearing monk's robes and holding a small medicine jar that represents his healing powers (**ill. 1**). In Tibet, he is sometimes depicted seated in his Lapis Lazuli Paradise, and in paintings he is generally coloured blue. He is usually shown with his right hand in the gift-giving mudra (41), and in his left is a medicine bowl or a myrobalan fruit, a five-sided lemon-like fruit with medicinal properties found in India and other tropical countries (**ill. 2**). In Japan, Bhaishajyaguru, or Yakushi, is often depicted flanked by two bodhisattvas, Suryaprabha (Japanese: Nikko, 'Splendour of the Sun') and Chandraprabha (Japanese: Gakko, 'Splendour of the Moon') in a representation known as the Bhaisajyaguru Triad, or Yakushi Sanzon (**ill. 3**). In some images of Bhaishajyaguru, the Healing Buddha is shown with seven small Buddhas on his aureole, a reference to the other seven Medicinal Buddhas.

Yaoshi (*Chinese*)
Yakushi (*Japanese*)
Yaksa (*Korean*)
Sangs-rgyas,
    Sman-bla
    (*Tibetan*)
Otochi
    (*Mongolian*)

1 Maitreya, schist, Gandhara, Pakistan, 3rd–4th century (left)

2 Seated Maitreya, gilt bronze, China, 16th–17th century (above)

3 Maitreya with crown in pensive pose, Korea, 7th century (below)

Identity

Maitreya, 'benevolence, friendship', is a unique figure in Buddhism as he is both a Buddha and a bodhisattva. He is believed to be the Buddha of the Future, successor of Shakyamuni (1), and is currently a bodhisattva waiting in the Tushita Heaven, where future Buddhas dwell, for the right time to appear as Buddha in this world. According to some Buddhist traditions, the period of the Buddhist Law is divided into three main stages: (1) The Turning of the Wheel of the Law (500 years); (2) The Deterioration of the Law (1,000 years); (3) The End of the Law (3,000 years), during which Buddhism is no longer practised. After this time Maitreya will appear in this world as a saviour figure and be enthroned by Shakyamuni as the next Buddha. His future status as a Buddha earns him the title 'Maitreya Buddha'.

Mile *(Chinese)*
Miroku
   (Japanese)
Mi-ruk *(Korean)*
Byams-pa
   (Tibetan)
Maijdari
   (Mongolian)
Di-lac
   (Vietnamese)

Principal Areas of Worship

Unlike many of the Buddhas and bodhisattvas of Mahayana Buddhism, Maitreya is also recognized by the Hinayana tradition of Buddhism as the Buddha-to-come. Images of Maitreya, usually depicted as a bodhisattva, exist in Java, Burma, Thailand, and other regions of Southeast Asia. In Tibet, he is a very popular bodhisattva, thought by many to be the founder of the Tantric School of Buddhism. According to tradition, the fourth century Indian sage, Asanga, visited Maitreya in the Tushita Heaven, and was taught the esoteric doctrine of the Tantra (which stresses mystical union with Buddhist deities), which he passed on after returning to earth. From the sixth century, this form of Buddhism evolved into the Vajrayana tradition of the Himalayan region.

In Korea and Japan, Maitreya enjoyed popularity around the sixth century as a saviour figure preparing to save the Buddhist world. A version of Maitreya is also worshipped in China, Japan and areas of Southeast Asia as the round Happy Buddha, a figure that has absorbed elements of lucky folk gods.

Representations and Attributes

Since Maitreya is Buddha of the Future, he is usually depicted as a bodhisattva wearing a crown and jewelry, indicating his current attachment to the world. In early images from Gandhara (in modern Pakistan, Afghanistan and northwestern India), Maitreya wears a robe resembling a Roman toga, and stands or sits regally with one hand in the fearlessness gesture (41) (**ill. 1**). In some Chinese, Southeast Asian, and other images, Maitreya sits on a throne with one or both legs pendant (**ill. 2**). In early Gandharan as well as East Asian sculptures, Maitreya sits with his right leg crossing over his left, his right hand touching his cheek and the elbow resting on his knee in a contemplative pose that suggests his presence in the Tushita Heaven waiting to appear as the Buddha (**ill. 3**). In some of these images, he is shown with one of his principal attributes, a small stupa in his headdress. In Himalayan images, Maitreya is an elegant bodhisattva, crowned and bejewelled and seated in the lotus posture. He often wears a scarf around his waist, and an antelope skin over his left shoulder.

1 Vairochana at the centre of the Diamond World, embroidered silk, Japan, 20th century (above left)

2 Vairochana at the centre of the Womb World, embroidered silk, Japan, 20th century (below left)

3 Vairochana making fist of wisdom, Japan (above)

Identity

Vairochana, 'The Illuminator', has the most complex identity of all the Buddhas. An important figure in esoteric Buddhist teachings, he is commonly considered first among the Five Dhyani Buddhas, transcendent beings who are also known as the Five Jinas, or 'conquerors', and the Five Tathagatas, or 'those who have come'. The number five possibly represents the five directions (four cardinal points and the zenith), the five significant moments in the life of the Buddha, or the five senses. These Buddhas represent the essence of the Buddha and his teachings. Vairochana is believed to dwell in Arupadhatu, the Heaven Beyond Form. Vairochana is considered by many Buddhists, particularly in Japan, to be the Supreme Buddha or the Cosmic Buddha, the embodiment of the Historical Buddha and his dharma. In certain schools of Northern Buddhism, Vairochana also corresponds to the Adi Buddha, a primordial, omniscient Buddha, who created the universe, and all other Buddhas.

Principal Areas of Worship

Vairochana is the principal Buddha of the esoteric teachings of Northern Buddhism, and is primarily worshipped in Nepal, Tibet, China and Japan. In Japan, Vairochana is considered to be the Cosmic Buddha, his infinite radiance giving him the title Dainichi, or Great Sun. He is also believed to be the originator of the esoteric Shingon school of Buddhism, a form of Tantric Buddhism, which emphasizes mystical spiritual union with certain Buddhist deities. In this tradition, Vairochana is the unifier of the two parts of the worlds: the spiritual and masculine Diamond World (Sanskrit: Vajradhatu) and the material and feminine Womb World (Sanskrit: Garbhadhatu). These worlds are represented visually in the Mandalas of the Two Worlds, in which Vairochana is the central figure.

Representations and Attributes

As one of the Dhyani Buddhas and the embodiment of the Buddhist Law, Vairochana is depicted as a monk-like Buddha sitting with his hands in gesture representing the setting of the Buddhist Law in motion (42). In the Japanese Shingon school Mandalas of the Two Worlds, Vairochana is depicted as a bodhisattva with a high crown and elaborate jewelry. In the Diamond World Mandala, Vairochana, sits at the centre of the four other Dhyani Buddhas, his hands forming the mudra of Six Elements (**ill. 1**). In the Womb World Mandala, he is at the heart of an eight-petalled lotus flower, representing the source of all life, his hands in the meditational dhyana mudra, the tips of his thumbs touching (**ill. 2**). The mudra of the Six Elements, or the Fist of Wisdom (44), is unique to Vairochana and represents the union of the two worlds, his left index finger representing the Diamond World, enveloped by the five fingers of the right hand, representing the Womb World (**ill. 3**). In Tibet and Nepal, Vairochana embraces his female consort, Locana or Vajradharisvari, in the yab-yum, or 'father-mother' attitude (40).

Palushena
  (Chinese)
Dainichi,
  Birushana
  (Japanese)
Pirojana (Korean)
Rnam-par-
  snang-mdsad
  (Tibetan)
Masi Geigulun
  Djogiaqchi
  (Mongolian)

1 Seated Akshobhya, Phitsanulok, Thailand (above)

2 The Buddha of Unshakable Resolve (Akshobhya) in his Eastern Paradise (Abhirati), opaque watercolor and gold on cotton, Western Tibet (Guge), 15th century (left)

3 Seated Akshobhya clutching robe, Japan (below)

Identity

Akshobhya, 'the Imperturbable', is the second of the five Dhyani Buddhas, and represents the element air. This Buddha is said to have expressed a wish never to experience strong emotions such as anger or repulsion and to remain undisturbed in order to achieve any task he set himself. He corresponds very closely to the Historical Buddha (1), Siddhartha Gautama, at the moment of enlightenment, when he called the earth to witness that he was unperturbed by the distractions sent by the evil King Mara. Akshobhya is believed to inhabit the Eastern Paradise of Abhiriti, as opposed to Amitabha's (6) Western Paradise. This belief has led to his being replaced in some Buddhist traditions by Bhaishajyaguru (2), who also resides in an Eastern Paradise.

Principal Places of Worship

Although Akshobhya was mentioned in several early sutras and is known in most Buddhist cultures, he has never achieved the great popularity of Buddhas such as Vairochana (4) and Amitabha, perhaps because he does not have as distinct a character or function as the others. In Tibet, he is worshipped as a Dhyani Buddha and represented as Shakyamuni, or Gautama Buddha, and appears in paintings and mandalas, but rarely in sculptures. In Southeast Asia, Buddhists of the Southern Tradition worship Akshobhya as Shakyamuni, the Historical Buddha. In China and Japan, he was venerated briefly, but in Japan has remained only as one of the Dhyani Buddhas in the mandalas of the Shingon school, and as one of the Thirteen Buddhas.

Representations and Attributes

Akshobhya is rarely venerated outside the group of five Dhyani Buddhas, so is rarely depicted as a single deity. This Buddha appears in the Japanese mandalas of Shingon Buddhism, in which he is one of the four Dhyani Buddhas surrounding Vairochana. In these images, he is a seated Buddha wearing a monk's robe and no ornamentation, and is painted gold or blue. He sits cross-legged with the soles of his feet facing upwards, often clutching the fold of his robe in his left hand, while his right hand is held palm upwards in the gift-giving gesture (41) and his right hand in the earth-touching mudra (43) associated with Shakyamuni (ill. 3). In Tibetan imagery, Akshobhya is sometimes represented in his Abhirati Paradise, seated and touching the earth with his right hand and with a vajra in his left hand or in front of him on his lotus seat (ill. 2). He is sometimes depicted in the yab-yum attitude (40) with his consort, Mamaki or Locana, holding a vertical vajra in his right hand and a bell in his left, while she holds a skull cap in her left hand. Akshobhya occasionally appears in Southeast Asian sculptural renditions of the Five Dhyani Buddhas, such as the eighth century group of stone figures in Borobodur, Java (81). In Thai representations, Akshobhya closely resembles Shakyamuni, and is generally depicted with his right hand touching the earth and his left hand in the meditation gesture (ill. 1).

Achu (*Chinese*)
Ach'ok (*Korean*)
Ashuku (*Japanese*)
Mi-bskyod-pa,
Mi-khrugs-pa
   (*Tibetan*)
Ulu Kudeluki
   (*Mongolian*)
Jinarat (*Thai*)

1 Seated Amitabha in Meditation Pose, Japan (above left)

2 Amitabha and attendants, Avalokiteshvara and Mahasthamaprapta, hand coloured woodblock print, Japan, 18th–19th century (above)

3 Amitabha and attendants in welcoming descent over the mountains, embroidered silk, Japan, 20th century (left)

Identity

Amitabha, the Buddha of 'Infinite Light', or Amitayus, the Buddha of 'Infinite Life', is the Buddha of the beyond and the afterlife, and is the fourth of the Five Dhyani Buddhas. He is one of the most compassionate figures in Buddhism and is believed to reside in Sukhavati, the Pure and Happy Land, a Buddhist paradise in the West. According to the *Sutra of the Pure and Happy Land*, all mortals can be reborn in this Pure Land if they worship Amitabha. This saving aspect of Amitabha originates from a vow made while still a bodhisattva to save all beings if he himself could attain enlightenment. Some scholars have identified this Buddha, with his links to the west and to the sun, with the ancient Persian god, Mithras, but this connection has not been proven.

Principal Areas of Worship

Although Amitabha appeared in Indian Buddhist texts in the early centuries AD, he was not a principal figure of worship there. In Southeast Asia, he was worshipped as one of the Five Dhyani Buddhas for a time, but was not worshipped as an individual Buddha. In China, he became the central figure of worship in the Pure Land school of Buddhism, in which it was promised that worship of this Buddha alone guaranteed rebirth in his paradise. He was worshipped to some degree both in China and in Korea, but it was in Japan where he gained his largest following. The simplicity of his doctrine and his compassionate nature made him extremely popular there, and from the ninth century onwards, he has been the most popular of all Buddhas. His promise of salvation to all mortals, irrespective of sex or social class, gave him enormous appeal among women and the lower classes. In the eighth century, Padmasambhava (29) introduced him in Tibet, where he gained popularity in Tantric Buddhism.

Representations and Attributes

In most depictions of Amitabha, he is seated in the lotus position with his hands on his lap in a meditational pose (43) with fingers and thumbs touching (**ill. 1**). In Himalayan Buddhism, Amitabha is often depicted seated wearing beautiful robes and jewels, flanked by his two bodhisattva attendants, Avalokiteshvara (8), representing the compassion of Amitabha, and Mahasthamaprapta, representing the wisdom of Amitabha (see p. 172). Avalokiteshvara often wears a tiny image of Amitabha in his headdress (see p. 42). In Tibet, China and Japan, Amitabha is often shown with these attendants in his palace in the Western Paradise, portrayed as a gorgeous garden full of celestial beings (**ill. 2**). In these images, Amitabha is generally depicted sitting in front of a Chinese-style palace looking out over a pond full of lotuses, onto which the souls of the devoted are reborn. In Japan, a particularly popular image known as a raigo shows Amitabha descending with his attendants, or sometimes an entire celestial entourage, to greet the soul of a deceased worshipper and transport it to be reborn in his Western Paradise (**ill. 3**).

Amida (*Japanese*)

Amituo (*Chinese*)

Amita (*Korean*)

Hod-dpag-med
(*Tibetan*)

Caghlasi ugei
gereltu
(*Mongolian*)

Phat Adida
(*Vietnamese*)

1 Seated Ratnasambhava, Java, c. 800 (top)

2 Seated Ratnasambhava, Tibet (centre left)

3 Seated Amoghasiddhi, Japan, Edo period (below left)

4 Seated Amoghasiddhi, bronze/copper/silver, Tibet 13th–14th century (below right)

Identity

Ratnasambhava, 'The Source of Precious Things', or 'He who is born of the Jewel', is the third and least popular of the Five Dhyani Buddhas, and represents the element fire. He has never been worshipped as an independent Buddhist deity, and images of him alone, particularly sculptures, are extremely rare. He is the Buddha of the south. This Buddha has been worshipped only as one of the Five Dhyani Buddhas in both the Northern and Southern traditions of Buddhism.

Representations and Attributes

Ratnasambhava only appears with the other four Dhyani Buddhas, most often in mandalas. He is generally depicted as a Buddha in a monk's robe with no ornamentation, seated in the lotus position, with the soles of his feet showing (**ill. 1**). In Tibetan representations, however, he is a crowned and bejewelled bodhisattva-like figure, his right hand forming the gesture of gift-giving (41), while his left hand holds the precious jewel (49) of Buddhism, or occasionally the fold of his robe (**ill. 2**). In the Diamond World Mandala of Japanese Shingon Buddhism, he is painted gold or yellow and is occasionally attended by four bodhisattvas. In some Tibetan depictions, he embraces his consort, Mamaki, and clasps a jewel in his right hand and a bell in his left, while she holds a skull cup in her left hand.

Baosheng *(Chinese)*
Posaeng *(Korean)*
Hosho *(Japanese)*
Rin-chen-hbyung
  (Tibetan)
Erdeni-in Oron
  (Mongolian)

Amoghasiddhi

Identity

Amoghasiddhi, 'The Unfailingly Successful' or 'He who works not in vain', is the fifth of the Five Dhyani Buddhas and represents the element earth. Like Ratnasambhava, this Buddha has never been the object of independent worship. His direction is the north. This Buddha has been worshipped only as one of the Five Dhyani Buddhas, in both the Northern and Southern traditions of Buddhism.

Representations and Attributes

Amoghasiddhi is only depicted with the other four Dhyani Buddhas as a group or in mandalas, in which he is usually painted green. He is shown as a seated Buddha in monk's robes, closely resembling Shakyamuni (1) in dress and hand gestures. In the Womb World Mandala, his hands are hidden in his robe (**ill. 3**), while in the Diamond World Mandala, his right hand touches the earth and his left hand is closed on his lap. In Tibet, he is often depicted as a bodhisattva-like being wearing a crown and jewels (**ill. 4**). He sometimes appears in yab-yum embrace (40) with his consort, or shakti (25), Tara (9), and holds a four-fold vajra in the right hand and a bell in the left.

Bukong chengjiu
  (Chinese)
Fukujoju *(Japanese)*
Don-grub *(Tibetan)*

1 Standing Avalokiteshvara with lotus, woodblock print, Japan, 19th century (right)

2 Head of Avalokiteshvara, wood, China 13th century (left)

3 Standing Avalokiteshvara as Goddess of Mercy, Perfume Pagoda, North Vietnam (below)

淺草寺

金龍山

Identity

Avalokiteshvara is probably the most popular and the most complex figure of worship in Buddhism. This bodhisattva appeared early in the texts and imagery of Mahayana Buddhism in India, where he gained a large following as an infinitely compassionate being. Also known as Lokeshvara, 'Lord of the World' or Lokanatha, 'Protector of the World,' he is the subject of the twenty-fourth chapter of the *Lotus Sutra*, in which he is described as looking in all directions in order to attempt to save all beings from the suffering of the world. He is believed to reside in the Potalaka Paradise.

Avalokiteshvara is the Dhyani bodhisattva who corresponds with the Buddha Amitabha (6), and certain legends claim that he was born from a ray of light emanating from the right eye of Amitabha. In East Asia in particular, Avalokiteshvara is believed to accompany Amitabha when the latter greets the souls of deceased devotees and transports them to paradise. The gender of Avalokiteshvara varies according to the spiritual needs of different cultures. In East Asia, Avalokiteshvara has a more feminine character and physique, while in most other Buddhist cultures, he is worshipped as a male bodhisattva.

Principal Places of Worship

Avalokiteshvara is worshipped throughout the Buddhist world, in the Mahayana and Vajrayana Buddhist cultures of the Himalayan region and East Asia in particular. The cult of Avalokiteshvara travelled to Nepal and Tibet in the first millennium. There, the compassionate bodhisattva was worshipped by practitioners of Vajrayana Buddhism in a male form, but often with his female counterpart, Tara (9). Over the centuries in Tibet, several compassionate kings and spiritual leaders have been regarded as incarnations of this bodhisattva, including the Dalai Lamas, who are believed to be Avalokiteshvara in human form.

Worship of Avalokiteshvara also travelled from India to Southeast Asia in the first millennium within the context of Vajrayana Buddhism. For centuries, he enjoyed popularity in Java and Sumatra in Indonesia, Vietnam, Cambodia, and Thailand. In China, Korea, and Japan, this bodhisattva has enjoyed more popularity than any other Buddhist figures, not only as a compassionate saviour, but also as a mother figure and a bestower of children. In Japan in the seventeenth century when Christianity was prohibited, Japanese Christians substituted images of Avalokiteshvara for those of the Virgin Mary in order to continue their worship.

Representations and Attributes

Avalokiteshvara has the largest number of representations of all the Buddhist figures. Traditionally, there are thought to be a total of 33 forms of Avalokiteshvara, the simplest being that of a bodhisattva holding a lotus (48), his principal attribute (**ill. 1**). The hand gesture most often associated with Avalokiteshvara is that of charity or gift giving (41). He also holds a water container (59), which he uses to relieve the thirst of his devotees (**ill. 3**). In many representations of Avalokiteshvara, he wears a small

Guanyin (*Chinese*)
Kannon (*Japanese*)
Kwanum (*Korean*)
Spyan-ras-gzigs (*Tibetan*)
Nidubarusheckchi (*Mongolian*)
Quan-am (*Vietnamese*)

4 Avalokiteshvara as attendant of Amitabha, Japan, 17th–18th century (top)

5 Eleven-headed Avalokiteshvara, gilt bronze, Tibet, 18th–19th century (top right)

6 One-thousand-armed Avalokiteshvara, gilt bronze, China, 16th century (right)

7 Seated Avalokiteshvara, porcelain, China, 19th century (above)

image of Amitabha in his headdress or crown (**ill. 2**). In Japan and China, the forms are the most diverse, and usually involve varying numbers of heads and arms, depending on the character of the particular forms of the bodhisattva.

Most Common Forms

Avalokiteshvara as attendant to Amitabha

In East Asia, Avalokiteshvara is often worshipped as an acolyte of Amitabha, and in paintings and prints is depicted with the bodhisattva, Mahasthamaprapta, flanking Amitabha as they descend from Amitabha's paradise to receive the souls of deceased devotees. Typically, Amitabha is shown descending on a cloud or a lotus, and Avalokiteshvara is kneeling in front of the other figures holding a lotus seat on which to carry the soul to Amitabha's Western Paradise (72) (**ill. 4**).

Eleven-headed Avalokiteshvara

In one of the most common esoteric forms of Avalokiteshvara, the bodhisattva has a total of eleven heads (**ill. 5**). The principal head is usually surmounted by three rows of three smaller heads crowned by a single head. The eleven heads symbolize the bodhisattva's principal virtues, which he uses to conquer the eleven desires that can obstruct the attainment of enlightenment. The uppermost head or standing figure represents the Buddha Amitabha, to whom he is closely related.

One thousand-armed Avalokiteshvara

Another esoteric form of Avalokiteshvara shows the bodhisattva with 1,000 arms, of which 42 or so are usually arranged like a fan around his body. These arms symbolize his many powers, which he uses to save all beings and lead them towards enlightenment. The central pair of arms are usually depicted in the gesture of praying, anjali mudra (44), and the outer arms may hold different attributes, representing the bodhisattva's various powers (**ill. 6**). The hands are often adorned with eyes, that symbolize the bodhisattva's omniscience and ability to see in all directions and assist all beings in their suffering.

Avalokiteshvara as Mother Figure or Bestower of Children

In China, Japan, and Vietnam, Avalokiteshvara is usually worshipped as a feminine deity, the Goddess of Mercy, with a female face and female robes (**ill. 7**). She was often depicted with breasts and holding a child, and in southern China and Japan, where Christianity was introduced by Europeans from the sixteenth century, a relationship grew between the Buddhist compassionate figure of Avalokiteshvara and the Christian compassionate Virgin and Child. Their images were often interchangeable.

1 Tara, gilt copper with polychrome and semiprecious stones, Nepal, c. 1300(left)

2 Green Tara, Tibet (above)

3 Green Tara surrounded by smaller Green Tara figures, painting on silk (detail), Tibet, 17th century (below)

Identity

Tara, 'She who helps to cross' or 'She who saves', is one of the pre-eminent female figures in Buddhism, and since around the sixth century AD has generally been revered as a female counterpart of the compassionate bodhisattva, Avalokiteshvara (8). Some legends claim that when Avalokiteshvara was looking down from his heaven at the world of suffering and weeping at his inability to save all beings from pain, the goddess Tara was born from his tears, or from a lotus floating in one of his tears. In some versions of this legend, two Taras were born from the tears, a peaceful white Tara from Avalokiteshvara's right eye, and a fierce green Tara from his left. Just as Avalokiteshvara represents the compassion of all of the Buddhas, and Manjushri (12) represents their wisdom, the bodhisattva Tara represents all of the miracles of the Buddhas of the past, present, and future. As such, these two Taras instilled Avalokiteshvara with the courage to continue his acts of compassion.

Principal Places of Worship

Tara is worshipped primarily in Tibet and Nepal within the context of Northern Buddhism. Among the Southern schools, rare images of her exist from Sri Lanka and Java. In Tibet, Tara was believed to be reincarnated in pious women, and in the seventh century, she was thought to have been reincarnated as the two wives – one Chinese, the other Nepali – of the Tibetan King Srong-btsan Sgam-po. The Tibetans, therefore, created two Taras – White Tara for the Chinese wife and Green Tara for the Nepali wife. Tara is also believed to have inspired the Bengali monk, Atisha, to travel to Tibet in the eleventh century AD and to renew Buddhism there.

Representations and Attributes

In painting and sculpture Tara is often represented as a beautiful bodhisattva standing in a swaying pose (**ill. 1**). Typically, she holds her right hand in the gift-giving gesture (41), while her left hand holds a lotus (48). Tibetan Buddhism has at least five differently coloured Taras – green, white, red, yellow, and blue – which represent her different aspects and correspond to the Five Dhyani Buddhas. The two most common forms are White Tara and Green Tara. White Tara, who symbolizes transcendent knowledge and purity, is one of the more serene forms of this bodhisattva, and is usually shown seated in full lotus position with her right hand in the wish-granting gesture and her left hand in the explanation mudra (42) and holding a lotus. Green Tara is Tara's most dynamic form and is frequently shown seated on a lotus throne (36) in the half lotus position (38), her right leg extended forward symbolizing her readiness to leap into action and save others (**ill. 2**). Her green colour associates her with the Buddha Amoghasiddhi (7), who is believed to transform the green poison of envy into the positive energy of wisdom. She holds a blue lotus. In some Tibetan paintings, a large central image of Green Tara is surrounded by hundreds of smaller images, symbolizing her omnipresence and infinite power to save other beings (**ill. 3**).

Tuoluo (*Chinese*)
Tarani, Tara
 (*Japanese*)
Sgrol-ma
 (*Tibetan*)
Dara eke
 (*Mongolian*)

1 Seated Akashagarbha, Tibet (left)

2 Seated Akashagarbha with sword and jewel, Japan (below)

Identity

Akashagarbha, 'He who encompasses space', is one of the Eight Bodhisattvas, but is less commonly worshipped and depicted than many of the others. According to certain sutras, his role is to destroy obstacles and help followers recover from their errors and practise the 'six perfections' or paramita, of Buddhism. He is also known as the 'guardian of infinite treasures', and is considered, along with Acalanatha (21), to be one of the two guardians of the Cosmic Buddha, Vairochana (4).

Principal Areas of Worship

Of the Eight Bodhisattvas, Akashagarbha is one of the least venerated, and there are apparently no extant images of him from India or Southeast Asia. In Tibet, China, and Japan, where he was once deeply venerated within the esoteric traditions, worship declined over the centuries, and images are rather rare. In Japan, he was one of the earliest bodhisattvas to be venerated and represented in sculpture. He is now mostly worshipped within the context of Shingon esoteric Buddhism in Japan, and is one of the deities represented in the Mandalas of the Two Worlds, though not a major figure. However, he is also worshipped in Japan as the Buddhist manifestation of the Japanese Shinto deity of Mount Asama in Shizuoka prefecture near Tokyo.

Representations and Attributes

Images of Akashagarbha are relatively rare. Those from the Tibetan Buddhist tradition depict him as a bodhisattva, crowned and bejewelled, either standing or sitting on a lotus throne and holding a precious jewel (49) and a lotus (48) (**ill. 1**). Images of this bodhisattva are more often confined to certain mandalas of the esoteric schools of Buddhism, in particular the Shingon tradition of Japan. Here, he is depicted as one of the Eight Bodhisattvas who typically surround the major deities of Mahayana Buddhism and wears a crown, jewelry and flowing robes and sashes. In the Mandala of the Womb World, he is typically shown seated holding a sword in his right hand representing his radiant wisdom and in his left hand a lotus on which is placed a precious jewel (**ill. 2**). On his head is a crown containing the images of the Five Dhyani Buddhas, Vairochana, Akshobhya (5), Amitabha (6), Amoghasiddhi (7), and Ratnasambhava (7) (**ill. 1**). In the Mandala of the Diamond World, he is depicted in five different forms, each representing contemplative aspects of the same Five Dhyani Buddhas. He is usually shown holding a lotus or a precious jewel in one hand, and a sword, elephant goad, or spear in the other.

In Japanese images of this bodhisattva, Akashagarbha is often considered a Buddhist manifestation of a particular Shinto mountain deity. The most common example of this is the image of Akashagarbha from Mount Asama, where he is worshipped as a Buddhist aspect of the Shinto deity, Asama Daimyojin. He is often shown flanked by the two Shinto deities, Amaterasu, the Sun Goddess, and her brother, Susa-no-o, the Storm God.

Xugongzang
  (Chinese)
Kokuzo
  (Japanese)
Nam-mka'i-
  snying-po
  (Tibetan)
Oqtarghui-in
  Jiruken
  (Mongolian)

1 Seated Kshitigarbha, Tibet (above left)

2 Kshitigharbha with staff and jewel, woodblock print (detail), Japan, 15th century (above)

3 Kshitigarbha rescuing souls in Hell, hand-coloured woodblock print (detail), Japan, 19th century (below left)

4 Group of stone Jizo figures, Buddhist temple cemetery, Japan, 20th century (below)

Dizang *(Chinese)*
Chijang *(Korean)*
Jizo *(Japanese)*
Sai-snying-po
   (Tibetan)
Gachar-un Jiruken
   (Mongolian)

Identity

Kshitigarbha, 'He who encompasses the Earth', is an important bodhisattva who is most well known for his vow to save all beings from the torments of Hell during the interim between the passing of the Buddha Shakyamuni (1) and the arrival of the Future Buddha Maitreya (3). In certain sutras, this bodhisattva is said to be the reincarnation of a young woman whose mother died slandering Buddhism and thus descended into Hell. The young woman, with the help of the Buddha, visited Hell and released her mother, but was so distressed by the suffering of the other souls there that she vowed to save them all. Kshitigarbha is often considered as the overlord of Hell, more powerful than Yama (15), King of Hell. He is also known as Master of the Six Realms of Rebirth (70), that is the realms of humans, gods, animals, the warlike beings known as *ashuras* (26), hungry ghosts, and hell.

Principal Places of Worship

Although Kshitigarbha was known in India as early as the fourth century, he was never a popular figure of worship in India, or in the Himalayan Tantric schools. Neither was he associated with Hell in these regions. In East Asia, however, he was worshipped from an early date as the 'good' judge over Hell, and was believed to rule over Yama and the nine other Kings or Judges of Hell. In this capacity, he was believed to be able to save souls from the punishments issued by these ten infernal judges. He was also worshipped by women with ugly faces who hoped for beauty in their next lives. In Japan, where he is most popular, images of him are often commissioned by bereaved parents in the hope of relieving their deceased children's labours along the banks of the Sai-no-Kawara River, similar to the mythical Greek River Styx, where they are forced by the Old Hag of Hell to pile up stones for eternity. Kshitigarbha is also believed to aid women wishing to conceive, and is the patron deity of travellers.

Representations and Attributes

In Tibetan imagery, Kshitigarbha usually appears as one of the Eight Bodhisattvas, and is represented as a crowned, bejewelled bodhisattva figure sitting on a lotus and holding a sacred jewel (49) in his right hand and forming the gift-giving (41) gesture with his left (**ill. 1**). In East Asia, Kshitigarbha is most often represented as a Buddhist monk, with a shaved head, monk's robe, and carrying in his right hand a staff, which was originally used by travelling monks to scare off snakes (**ill. 2**). It is possible that this representation originates from the belief that this bodhisattva once appeared to the Buddha in the form of a priest. In his left hand, Kshitigarbha generally holds a sacred jewel of Buddhism. In Japanese Buddhist imagery, he is often shown in the form of a priest descending into the flames of Hell in order to rescue the souls of sufferers (**ill. 3**). However, probably the most commonly seen representations of this bodhisattva are the stone figures of Jizo in Japanese Buddhist cemeteries, which are erected as prayers to this bodhisattva to save the souls of deceased children and are dressed with the clothes of these children (**ill. 4**).

1 Seated Manjushri with sword, Japan, 18th century (above)

2 Manjushri astride a white lion, Japan (above right)

3 Manjushri (right) and Samantabhadra (left) flanking Shakyamuni, woodblock print, Japan, 19th century (below right)

Identity

Manjushri, 'The Beautiful, Virtuous Lord', is the bodhisattva most often associated with wisdom, specifically the wisdom of the Buddha, and is commonly paired with Samantabhadra (13), who represents his compassion. These two bodhisattvas are considered important acolytes of Shakyamuni (1), and are believed by some to have been historical figures, possibly disciples of the Buddha. Manjushri is often regarded as the master, parent and friend of all the bodhisattvas and the spiritual son of the Buddha. He resides in the East in the Vimala Paradise, and certain texts state that he lives on a five-peaked mountain in the Himalayas, while others state that his paradise is on a five-peaked mountain in China. According to Chinese Buddhist legends, he was created by Shakyamuni, the Historical Buddha, in order to save the Chinese from spiritual ignorance. Shakyamuni caused a golden ray to burst from his forehead and pierce a magical tree on the Wutaishan (Five-peaked Mountain) in Shanxi province. A lotus grew out of the tree and from inside the lotus appeared Manjushri.

Principal Places of Worship

Manjushri was the first bodhisattva to be mentioned in the Buddhist scriptures, in connection with Shakyamuni, and has since early times been a popular figure in both Northern and Southern Buddhism. From the fourth century AD, Manjushri has been associated with Wutaishan in China, which has since then been a major centre of worship and pilgrimage for his devotees. Many Chinese Buddhists believe that Manjushri was instructed by Shakyamuni to transmit his teachings to the Chinese. In Nepal, he is a supremely important bodhisattva and is celebrated on the first day of every year. He is believed by many to be the creator of Nepal and the initiator of civilization, but others believe that he was, in fact, a historical figure who brought Buddhism to Nepal. From around the eighth century AD, he has also been revered widely in Japan as the bodhisattva of wisdom, alongside Samantabhadra, bodhisattva of compassion.

Representations and Attributes

Manjushri, like most bodhisattvas, wears a crown, robes, and princely jewelry, and is often portrayed as a young boy with his hair tied in several chignons (usually five). He is identifiable by the sword he holds in his right hand to cut through ignorance, and a lotus or the *Prajnaparamita*, or *Perfection of Wisdom Sutra*, in his left hand, representing the knowledge of the Buddha (**ill. 1**). He often rides a white lion, whose roar symbolizes the voice of the Buddhist Law (**ill. 2**). Both he and Samantabhadra are often depicted flanking Shakyamuni, personifying his wisdom and compassion (**ill. 3**). In Tibetan yab-yum images (40), he either embraces his consort Sarasvati (24), Goddess of Learning, or holds her on his knee; in these images he has three or five heads and multiple arms. In Vajrayana Buddhist art, he is sometimes depicted as the wrathful protector deity, Yamantaka (16), a fierce, buffalo-headed creature whose form Manjushri assumed in order to destroy Yama (15), the Lord of Death.

Wenshu *(Chinese)*
Munsu *(Korean)*
Monju *(Japanese)*
Jam-dpal *(Tibetan)*
Manchushri
   (Mongolian)

1 Samantabhadra riding white elephant, embroidered silk, Japan, 20th century (right)

2 Seated Samantabhadra making gesture of explanation, Vietnam (above)

3 Samantabhadra, Prolonger of Life, Japan (below)

Identity

Samantabhadra, 'Universal Knowledge and Bounty', represents compassion and the Law of the Buddha. He is often partnered with Manjushri (12), and together they are considered important acolytes of Shakyamuni (1), possibly once actual disciples of the Buddha. He is the first of the Five Dhyani Bodhisattvas, corresponding to the Five Dhyani Buddhas of Northern Buddhism. His direction is the East. In Tibet, he was worshipped for a time as the Adi Buddha, or Primordial Buddha, but this belief is now only held by followers of the Nyingma sect.

Principal Areas of Worship

Samantabhadra is venerated in both the Northern and Southern Buddhist traditions, but has never had a strong following as an individual deity. Some esoteric Himalayan schools claim that this bodhisattva, and not Vairochana, was the founder of the Tantric school of mystical Buddhism, in which devotees seek to form a mystical union with deities. In China, Samantabhadra is almost always worshipped with Shakyamuni and Manjushri, and is believed to reside on a mountain in Sichuan province. In Japan, Samantabhadra has a strong following in the Tendai, Shingon and Nichiren sects, where he is considered the Patron of the *Lotus Sutra*. In Japan and other areas, he is also worshipped in the esoteric form of Samantabhadra, the 'Prolonger of Life.'

Representations and Attributes

Samantabhadra usually appears in a triad with Shakyamuni and Manjushri. He stands to the right of Shakyamuni, and Manjushri is on the left, and they are occasionally surrounded by the Sixteen Good Spirits who protect the *Prajnaparamita Sutra*, the *Sutra of the Perfection of Wisdom*. He generally appears as a bodhisattva with a crown and princely robes and jewelry, and in many images rides on a single- or many-headed elephant (**ill. 1**). His principal attribute is the sacred jewel (49), which he usually holds in his left hand or which sits on a lotus, the stem of which he holds in his left hand. In many representations, one of his hands forms the explanation mudra (42), with thumb and index finger touching in a triangular pose (**ill. 2**). In other images, he holds a scroll or a mace, or baton, or even a vajra in his left hand. In Japanese images of Samantabhadra as the 'Prolonger of Life,' he is shown with twenty arms and is seated on a four-headed white elephant or on four white elephants (**ill. 3**).

In esoteric Buddhist paintings, his colour is green or yellow. In images of the Tibetan Nyingma order, Samantabhadra, as the Adi Buddha, is depicted in yab-yum embrace at the centre of the Shi-tro Mandala, the mandala of the peaceful and wrathful deities of the one hundred Buddha families, a mandala that is created in order to create universal peace (73). However, this same peaceful Adi Buddha is represented in a wrathful form known as Chemchok Heruka. In this form, he is a winged figure with a dark reddish brown body, three faces, six arms and four legs, and is usually depicted in sexual embrace with his bright red consort.

Puxian *(Chinese)*
Pohyon *(Korean)*
Fugen *(Japanese)*
Kun-tu bzang-po
   (Tibetan)
Qamugha Sain
   (Mongolian)
Pho-hien
   (Vietnamese)

1 Seated Vajrapani, Tibet (above)

2 Vajrapani as a Wrathful Protector Deity, bronze, Tibet, 16th century (below)

3 Chana Dorje and his Consort, gilt copper with paint, Central Tibet, 15th century (right)

Kingang (*Chinese*)
Kongo (*Japanese*)
Chana Dorje,
 Phyag-na rdo-rje
(*Tibetan*)
Vachirpani
 (*Mongolian*)

Identity

Vajrapani, 'the Holder of the Vajra' (55), is the bodhisattva who represents the power of all the Buddhas, just as Avalokiteshvara (8) represents their compassion, Manjushri (12) their wisdom, and Tara (9) their miraculous acts. To many Buddhists, Vajrapani represents removal of obstacles and the conquest of negativity through fierce determination, symbolized by the vajra that he holds. As one of the Five Dhyani Bodhisattvas of esoteric Buddhism, he is closely associated with the Buddha Akshobhya (5).

In early legends, Vajrapani was described as the guardian of the nagas, or serpent deities, and protected them against their enemies, the garudas, bird-like deities. He is considered the guardian of the Elixir of Life, appearing occasionally alongside Amitayus (6). In one legend, the Buddhas tried to hide poison from evil demons who were trying to destroy mankind. They charged Vajrapani with guarding the poison while they searched for the antidote, the sweet liquid amrita, but Vajrapani allowed the poison to be stolen by a demon. The gods punished him by making him drink water contaminated by the poison, which turned him blue.

Principal Places of Worship

Vajrapani is worshipped primarily in the Himalayan region in tantric Buddhist practices. Though a bodhisattva, he is chiefly considered to be the implacable conqueror of demons, and is often worshipped as a fierce protector deity. Since the *nagas* guard the rain clouds, Vajrapani, as their protector, was often worshipped as the Rain God. He is also venerated as a protector against snakes and snake bites. In China and Japan, he is not widely worshipped and only appears in the mandalas of the esoteric schools. He has been worshipped to a small degree in areas of Southeast Asia, including Cambodia.

Representations and Attributes

Vajrapani appears in some Tibetan and Nepalese imagery as a bodhisattva who holds a vajra, usually in his right hand, and makes the gift-giving (41) gesture with his left hand. Sometimes the vajra rests on a lotus, the stem of which Vajrapani holds in his right hand. Vajrapani may also hold a vajra in one hand and a bell (58) in the other, representing the union of wisdom and compassion (**ill. 1**). In some images, a small seated figure of the Buddha Akshobhya is shown in his crown, symbolizing his ability to transform anger into wisdom. In Tibet, he often appears in his various tantric forms as a fearsome protector deity, with one or more human heads, wild hair, a third eye, and multiple arms and legs. He often wears a skull crown and a necklace of serpents. He always holds up a vajra in one of his right arms and usually stands leaning to the right (**ill. 2**). Vajrapani is often depicted embracing his female consort, Sujata, who represents wisdom uniting with his compassion (**ill. 3**). He stands on two prostrate figures, one beneath each foot, representing ignorance. In his six hands he holds vajras and snakes, who attack the figures below, and makes gestures of fearlessness, gift-giving, and explanation of the Buddhist Law.

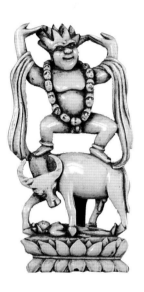

1 Yama Standing on a Bull, ivory, Sino-Tibetan, *c.* 1800 (above left)

2 Yama on a bull, Tibet (left)

3 Yama and sister, Yami, painting in colours on silk (detail), Tibet, *c.* 1700 (above)

4 Yama as King of Hell, Japan (right)

Identity

Yama, 'Lord of Death', is the buffalo-headed king of the dead, who was absorbed from ancient Indian beliefs into Buddhism as one of the eight Dharmapalas, or protectors of the Buddhist Law. According to one legend, he was originally a king of Vaisali, in India. During a bloody war, he wished to become master of Hell, and was reborn as Yama in Hell with his generals and army. A Tibetan legend tells of two robbers who entered a cave with a stolen bull and killed it by chopping off its head. In the same cave was a holy man on the verge of attaining enlightenment. The robbers beheaded him too, but his body suddenly assumed the form of Yama, the King of Hell, and set the bull's head on its own shoulders. Yama then killed the robbers and drank their blood from cups made from their skulls. In his fury, he then threatened to kill the entire population of Tibet. The terrified Tibetans called upon the bodhisattva Manjushri (12) to save them. Manjushri transformed into Yamantaka (16) and destroyed Yama.

Yama is believed to reside in a palace of copper and iron at the extremity of the earth. When the wicked die, they travel 680,000 miles to his realm. In Buddhist tradition, there are numerous Hells (71), including eight hot and eight cold Hells. After being judged by Yama, the dead are led by demons to the hell most appropriate to their misdeeds. Yama is sometimes accompanied by his sister, Yami, who looks after female culprits.

Principal Areas of Worship

Yama is principally worshipped in Tibet and Nepal, where he is at once a Dharmapala and the King of the Dead. In Chinese Buddhism, there are a total of Ten Kings of Hell, and Yama is merely the fifth of these kings and is subordinate to Kshitigarbha (11). In Japan, he is the foremost of the Ten Kings and presides over the Hells.

Representations and Attributes

In Himalayan painting and sculpture, Yama is generally depicted with the head of a buffalo and a necklace of skulls, and often stands on the back of a buffalo (**ill. 1**). In Tibet, Yama assumes three principal forms: (1) A fierce, red deity with a buffalo's head and hair that rises up like flames. He stands on a buffalo and holds a chopper (57), or a precious jewel (49), and a skull cup (60) (**ill. 2**). He is often accompanied by two skeletons, known as chitipati, 'lords of the funeral pyre'. (2) Accompanied by his sister, Yami, he is dark blue and resembles Gsang-sgrub; when alone, he is white or yellow. In this form, he is the protector of the Tibetan Yellow Hat (Gelukpa) sect of Buddhism (**ill. 3**). (3) He is dark blue, holds a chopper and a skull cup, and stands on a man. In this form, he is a judge of hell.

In East Asian images, Yama is depicted as a middle-aged man with a powerful Indian face and a thick beard. He wears the long, flowing robes of a Chinese official and a judge's cap on his head. He is usually shown seated in the position of a judge, his right hand holding the mace of office (**ill. 4**).

Yanluo Wang
(Chinese)
Emma-O
(Japanese)
Chos-rgyal,
Gshin-rje
(Tibetan)
Erlig Khan
(Mongolian)

1 Yamantaka, embroidered silk, Japan, 20th century (left)

2 Yamantaka and consort on bull (below left)

3 Yamantaka and consort in yab-yum, painting in colours on silk (detail), Tibet, c. 1700 (below)

Identity

Yamantaka, 'Terminator of Death', is a wrathful manifestation of the bodhisattva Manjushri (12) and is one of the Dharmapalas, or Protectors of the Buddhist Law. He is one of the most complex of all the deities of Northern Buddhism and a major deity in certain sects of the Vajrayana Buddhist tradition. He is believed to represent the diamond-like wisdom of ultimate reality and victory over evil, suffering, and death. According to Buddhist legend, Yama (15), the buffalo-headed Lord of Death, was intent on killing the entire population of Tibet. The people of Tibet called upon the compassionate bodhisattva Manjushri to save them. Manjushri assumed Yama's fearsome buffalo-headed form and succeeded in destroying Yama, thus terminating death.

Principal Areas of Worship

Yamantaka is revered primarily in Tibet, where he is an extremely important wrathful deity among followers of the Gelukpa sect of Tibetan Buddhism. Yamantaka was highly significant in the life of Tsong Khapa (Yellow Hat, 1357–1419), the lama who is generally considered to have founded the Gelukpa sect and who was believed to be an incarnation of Manjushri. He is also venerated in Japan within the context of esoteric Shingon Buddhism, and in this sect is worshipped as an individual deity and as well as one of the Five Kings of Mystical Knowledge (21).

Representations and Attributes

In most paintings and sculptures of Yamantaka, the deity is represented as a fierce deity with six heads and six pairs of arms. The central head is usually a buffalo head crowned with skulls; he wears a necklace of skulls and has a third eye in the centre of his forehead (**ill. 2**). One of his other heads is usually that of the bodhisattva Manjushri, of whom he is a manifestation. In Japanese images, he is generally depicted as a blue-skinned wrathful deity seated on a bull, holding various weapons in his multiple hands, and surrounded by flames (**ill. 1**).

In Tibetan Buddhism, Yamantaka assumes three principal forms: (1) the multi-coloured Vajrabhairava (Diamond Terrifier), (2) the red Raktayamari, and (3) the black Krishnayamari. The most popular form of Yamantaka is Vajrabhairava, the 'Diamond Terrifier.' This wrathful form relates to the fierce Bhairava form of the Hindu god Shiva, who destroys the universe at the end of each cosmic cycle. In Tibetan Buddhism, aspects of Shiva and of Yamantaka have merged into the one important cult of Vajrabhairava Yamantaka, a wrathful deity who is often depicted with a buffalo head, fangs, a crown of skulls and several smaller heads, the central one of which represents Manjushri. Just as Shiva dances his cosmic dance on top of human figures representing ignorance, Vajrabhairava Yamantaka also tramples such figures beneath his many pairs of powerful feet. In certain images of Yamantaka, the deity is shown in yab-yum (father-mother embrace) with his consort, Vajravetali, the Diamond Zombie, who is pale blue in paintings (**ill. 2, 3**).

Yamandejia
  (Chinese)
Daiitoku-Myo-o
  (Japanese)
Gshin-rje-gshed
  (Tibetan)
Erlig-jin
  Jarghagchi
  (Mongolian)

1 Mahakala, Tibet (above)

2 Mahakala holding animal skin, trident, skull cup and other attributes, Tibet, 16th century (right)

3 Daikoku, Japan (below)

Dahei Wang
  (Chinese)
Daikoku,
  Makiakara
  (Japanese)
Mnon-po *(Tibetan)*
Yeke gara
  (Mongolian)

Identity

Mahakala, 'The Great Black One', is a fierce protector deity, who, in Tibet, is one of the eight Dharmapalas, or Protectors of the Buddhist Law, and is a Yidam (22), or Tibetan protector deity. He is also described as being the fierce form of the bodhisattva Avalokiteshvara (8), or a destructive form of the Hindu god, Shiva. According to the writings of a Chinese Buddhist pilgrim, images of a seated god holding a bag of gold were placed at the doorways of monasteries and were anointed with oil by worshippers. The oil turned the statues black, and so the figures were known as Mahakala, or 'Great Black One'. The bag of gold is an attribute of Kubera (19), the God of Wealth, so the deity may have originated as Kubera. In Nepal, images of Mahakala closely resemble Kubera and may be one and the same deity.

Principal Areas of Worship

Mahakala is worshipped as a fierce protector deity primarily in Tibet, Nepal, and Mongolia. In Tibet, because of his role as a protector deity, his image is often placed at the inner entrance of a temple. He was introduced to Mongolia under Tibetan influence in the sixteenth or seventeenth century, and since then has been the protector god of Mongolia. In Japan, he is worshipped as Daikoku or Makiakara-ten, the 'Great Black One' in esoteric Buddhism, but has been better known since the seventeenth century as the God of Wealth, one of the Seven Lucky Gods (Shichifukujin).

Representations and Attributes

Images of Mahakala are most common in the Buddhist art of Tibet and Mongolia. In most images, he is coloured black and is shown as a standing figure with six arms. In his two uppermost arms, he holds the feet of a flayed elephant skin, which he stretches out across his back (**ill. 2**). In the upper right hand he also holds a skull rosary (62) and in the upper left a trident. In his middle right hand he holds a hand drum (58), and the middle left hand holds a lasso. In front of his body, his two lower hands hold a chopper (57) and a skull bowl (60) containing a heart, symbolizing his power to destroy inner addictions and outer evil forces that obstruct the search for enlightenment. He may also be shown with other adornments characteristic of wrathful beings, including a necklace of skulls, a live snake cord draped around his neck, and an elephant goad, a bow, or other weapon (**ill. 1**).

In Japan, he is commonly seen as the God of Prosperity, Daikoku, a fat, smiling man carrying a bag of grain (or treasures or wisdom) over his shoulder and standing on two rice bales (**ill. 3**). This popular deity often wears a flat peasant's cap and carries a lucky mallet that he shakes to obtain riches.

1 Vaishravana, Guardian of the North, Japan (above)

2 Dhrtarastra, Guardian of the East, Japan (right)

3 Virudhaka, Guardian of the South, Japan (below)

4 Virupaksa, Guardian of the West, Japan (left)

Identity

The Four Heavenly Kings, or Lokapala, 'Guardian Kings', guard the four cardinal points of the world and are the Protectors of the Buddhist Law. Well known in Buddhism since the time of the Historical Buddha (1), they derived from earlier pre-Buddhist directional deities. According to Buddhist legends, these kings were present at every critical moment in the Buddha's life: they assisted with his birth; they carried Prince Siddhartha's horse's legs when he left his father's palace; they offered him food before his enlightenment; and they attended his parinirvana. Vaishravana (19) is the chief of the four and guards the North and winter. The other three are Dhrtarashtra, who guards the East and spring, Virudhaka, who guards the South and summer, and Virupaksha, guardian of the West and autumn.

Principal Places of Worship

The Four Heavenly Kings have been venerated throughout the Buddhist world from at least the second century BC, when their representations appeared on the four sides of stupas, such as the Great Stupa of Sanchi (75), guarding the Buddhist relics inside. They were also worshipped in Gandhara and Kashmir at a very early date. They gained a following in China and Central Asia around the eighth century as protectors of the Buddhist Law and of Buddhist rulers. In Japan, they were embraced at an early date by Buddhist clans to ensure victory against their enemies. In the sixth century, the ardent Buddhist prince Shotoku Taishi erected the Shitenno-ji temple in their honour. They are also worshipped in the Himalayan region, and in the Southern Tradition of Buddhism in Southeast Asia. Only Vaishravana is worshipped independently and he is closely associated with the god Kubera (19).

Representations and Attributes

In early Indian images, these kings are bare-breasted and carry lances. Later, these kings were represented as fierce warriors, carrying weapons and wearing armour decorated with a lion or demon head on the central section. As a group, they stand in dramatic poses, with one or both feet trampling demonic figures representing the enemies of Buddhism. Behind their heads are either flaming aureoles (36) or wheels (47), representing the Buddhist Law. Scarves billowing around their bodies represent their celestial nature.

The kings have distinct attributes. Vaishravana, 'He who is knowing', holds a stupa and a staff (**ill. 1**). Dhrtarastra, 'He who maintains the kingdom of the Law', is blue or green in China, corresponding to the Daoist blue dragon of the East, but in India and Tibet, he is white. He usually holds a sword in one hand (**ill. 2**). Virudhaka, 'He who enlarges the kingdom', is red in China, corresponding to the Daoist Red Phoenix of the South, but in Tibet is green. He holds either a sword or a lance (**ill. 3**). Virupaksha, 'He who observes all things in the kingdom', and in China is white, corresponding to the white tiger of the west. In Tibet and India, he is usually red. He often holds a lasso or a sutra (68) (**ill. 4**).

Sitian wang
  (Chinese)

Shi-Tenno
  (Japanese)

Sa Ch'onwang
  (Korean)

Lokapala
(Sanskrit)

Rgyal-chen-bhi
(Tibetan)

Maharaja
  (Mongolian)

1 Vaishravana holding staff and pagoda, wood, polychrome, Japan, 12th century (above left)

2 Vaishravana/Kubera on Lion, painting on silk, Tibet, 12th century (above)

3 Seated Kubera, gilded bronze, Tibet, 17th century (left)

4 Kubera squeezing mongoose (right)

Identity

Vaishravana, 'He who is knowing', or 'He who hears everything in the kingdom', is the chief of the Lokapala, or Four Heavenly Kings (18), and is the guardian of the North and of winter. In Tibet and Nepal, he is closely related to the God of Wealth, Kubera, who is considered to be his most important manifestation. It is possible that Vaishravana is the Buddhist form of the earlier Hindu deity, Kuvera/Kubera, who was the son of an Indian sage, Vishrava, hence the name, Vaishravana. According to Hindu legend, Kubera performed austerities for a thousand years, and was rewarded for this by the creator god, Brahma, who granted him immortality and the position of God of Wealth, and guardian of the treasures of the earth. As Vaishravana, this deity also commands the army of eight yakshas (26), or demons, who are all believed to be emanations of Vaishravana himself. The most important of these eight are the dark-skinned Kubera of the north and the white Jambala of the east. Each of these emanations holds a mongoose that spews jewels.

Principal Places of Worship

Vaishravana is the only one of the Four Guardian Kings to have been worshipped as an individual deity, and he was worshipped widely in India and Central Asia, and in most of the cultures that embraced the Northern Tradition of Buddhism. In Japan, he was worshipped independently of the other three guardian kings from around the ninth century, at which time, he was not only considered a god of warfare but as a healing god with the powers to heal emperors. Later, in the seventeenth century, in his capacity as a dispenser of wealth and good fortune, he became one of the Seven Lucky Gods, or Shichifukujin. In Tibet and Nepal, he has been worshipped as the God of Wealth in all three manifestations: Vaishravana, Kubera and Jambala.

Representations and Attributes

When he appears as Vaishravana, Guardian of the North, he wears armour and strikes a dramatic pose, with a lance in his right hand and a small stupa in his left (65) (**ill. 1**). This stupa is also described as a small treasure tower which Vaishravana guards. In sculptural form, Vaishravana usually appears with the three other guardian kings, each of whom stands in a ferocious pose at one corner of the Buddhist temple altar, protecting the main figure of worship in the centre of the altar.

In India, Tibet and Nepal, Vaishravana/Kubera is depicted as a corpulent figure, usually seated and either covered with jewels, or holding a bag full of jewels. He is often shown wearing a suit of armour riding a lion, and surrounded by his eight *yaksha* generals (**ill. 2**). In many Tibetan and Nepalese images of Kubera, the deity is shown as a plump figure wearing a crown, ribbons and jewelry and holding a mongoose, representing this god's victory over the nagas (54), or snake deities, who symbolize greed (**ill. 3**). As God of Wealth, Vaishravana/Kubera squeezes the mongoose and causes the creature to spew out jewels (**ill. 4**).

Duowen tian
  (*Chinese*)
Bishamon-ten,
  Tamon-ten
  (*Japanese*)
Damun ch'on
  (*Korean*)
Rnam Thos-kyi Bu,
  Rnam Thos-sras
  (*Tibetan*)
Bisman Tengri
  (*Mongolian*)

1 Guardian figure, wood, at temple entrance, Horyuji, Nara, Japan, 8th century (left)

2 Garbhavira, or Misshaku Rikishi (below left)

3 Vajravira, or Kongo Rikishi (below right)

Identity

At the entrance to Buddhist temples in East Asia, giant gate guardians stand on either side of the main southern gate to ward off evil spirits or thieves. These gate guardians are considered to be 'benevolent kings', or dvarapala, and together they protect the entrance of the temple, in much the same way as the Four Heavenly Kings (18) protect the Buddhist universe. They are believed by Buddhists to represent the two opposing forces of the universe. One holds his mouth open uttering the syllable, 'a'; the other has a closed mouth and murmurs 'um'. Together, these two sounds create the sacred sound of the cosmos: a-um, or Om.

Principal Areas of Worship

Although Indian in origin and Indian or Central Asian in appearance, with large noses and bulging eyes, these figures are found most frequently at the main gates of Japanese temples, although they also guard temples in China and Korea. These guardians are not objects of worship themselves but serve to protect the temple and its worshippers.

Representations and Attributes

These fierce-looking guardians are generally represented in pairs and usually wear only a loin cloth around their waists, exposing muscular arms and torsos. They either have shaved heads or wear a chignon on the top of their heads. Although some guardians exist in stone, they are usually carved out of wood (**ill. 1**), and, because of their awesome stature, are generally made from several pieces of wood joined together. Occasionally, they wear suits of armour and brandish weapons. Individually, the two guardians, Garbhavira and Vajravira have distinct characteristics.

Garbhavira (Japanese: Misshaku Rikishi)

Garbhavira, or the 'Womb with secret traces', is always placed to the east of the main gate of the temple, so to the right as one enters the temple. He strikes a dynamic pose, with one hand reaching downwards and the other hand grasping a staff with vajras (55) at each end. He often has his mouth open, making the more active sound 'a', which symbolizes the beginning of life (**ill. 2**). When painted, he is coloured red. In esoteric Buddhism, Garbhavira is the guardian of the Garbhadhatu Mandala, the Mandala of the Womb World (73) and symbolizes its power.

Vajravira (Japanese: Kongo Rikishi)

Vajravira, or the 'Vajra with secret traces,' is found to the west of the temple gate, on the left as one enters. Almost the mirror image of Garbhavira, he also strikes a dynamic pose, with one hand thrust downward and the other hand holding a staff with a vajra at each end. He has his mouth closed, making the more passive sound 'um', which symbolizes the end of life (**ill. 3**). When painted, his body is green. In esoteric Buddhism, he is the guardian of the Mandala of the Diamond World (73).

1 Acalanatha, Japan (above right)

2 Trailokyavijaya, embroidered silk, Japan, 20th century (above)

3 Ragavidyaraja, embroidered silk, Japan, 20th century (right)

Identity

The Kings of Mystical Knowledge, or Vidyarajas, are wrathful deities who represent the power of the Jinas, or transcendental Buddhas, over the passions. Although there are several such deities, there are five principal Kings of Mystical Knowledge, also known as Kings of Light, each one considered to be an emanation of one of the Five Dhyani Buddhas. Each of these kings also corresponds to the four directions (north, south, east, west) and centre of the Buddhist cosmos. The five principal Kings are Acalanatha, who corresponds to Vairochana (4) in the centre; Trailokyavijaya, who corresponds to Akshobhya (5) in the east; Kundali, who corresponds to Ratnasambava (7) in the south; Yamantaka (16), who corresponds to Amitabha (6) in the west; Vajrayaksha, corresponding to Amoghasiddhi (7) in the north.

Vidyaraja
(Sanskrit)
Ming wang
(Chinese)
Myo-O
(Japanese)
Myongwang
(Korean)

Principal Areas of Worship

The Kings of Mystical Knowledge are worshipped as individual deities in many esoteric traditions and in groups of five primarily in the esoteric Buddhist schools of Japan. Yamantaka is most commonly worshipped as an independent deity in the Himalayan region, as the destroyer of Yama (15), and the conqueror of death. Acalanatha, the wrathful emanation of Vairochana and the chief of the five Kings, has been the most popular wrathful deity in Japan, where he is known as Fudo Myo-O, the Immovable One, and symbolizes firmness of spirit and the determination to destroy evil. As a group, the five Kings of Mystical Knowledge are most commonly worshipped in Japan where, from the thirteenth century, they were transformed from esoteric deities to popular protector gods, guarding against evil forces.

Representations and Attributes

The Kings of Mystical Knowledge are depicted as wrathful deities with angry faces and fangs and often wearing animal skins and necklaces of skulls. They carry weapons such as swords, bows and arrows with which to destroy negative forces and passions. They are usually surrounded by flames which are believed to be able to consume the passions. The Kings are represented either as individual subjects of worship or in groups. As they are essentially esoteric beings and are wrathful emanations of the Five Dhyani Buddhas, they are often seen in groups in mandalas, where they are usually shown seated on lotuses, with Acalanatha in the centre.

Acalanatha probably has the strongest following, particularly in Japan, where he became a popular deity outside Buddhism. In his right hand, he holds a sword which he uses to combat the three poisons: greed, anger and ignorance. In his left hand he holds a rope with which he catches and binds up evil (**ill. 1**). Trailokyavijaya, 'Conqueror of the Three Worlds', triumphs over these three poisons using swords, arrows and other weapons. He is often shown trampling the Hindu god Shiva, who represents the passions, and his wife Parvati (**ill. 2**). The red king, Ragavidyaraja, 'Conqueror of the Passions', sits on a lotus throne and uses his various weapons to transform amorous desire into the desire for enlightenment (**ill. 3**).

1 Hevajra and consort, Nairatma, in yab-yum, Tibet (above)

2 Samvara and consort, Vajravarahi, in yab-yum, Tibet (below)

3 Kalachakra and consort, Vishvamata, painting in gouache on cotton, Tibet, 18th or 19th century (right)

A yidam is a Tibetan tutelary god, a deity adopted as a kind of guardian angel who may be called on at times of crisis. In theory, any deity in the Tibetan Buddhist pantheon can be adopted as a personal protector, so there are many yidams in Tibetan Buddhism. In fact, every monastery, family and individual is assigned a protector deity. An individual is assigned a yidam by a lama during initiation and carries an image of this deity with him in a portable shrine, often worn as a pendant. Many yidams are represented in their peaceful aspects, with the jewels and crowns of a bodhisattva, and most are shown in sexual embrace with their female counterparts, or shaktis (25). Some yidams, however, are wrathful deities wearing necklaces of skulls.

Hevajra

The deity Hevajra, 'Eternal Vajra', is worshipped principally in Tibet, Nepal, and Mongolia, and has also had a following in Thailand and Cambodia, but appears not to have been worshipped in East Asia. In Tibet, Hevajra is the yidam of the Sakyapa Buddhist order. He is usually depicted as a peaceful deity dancing or standing in sexual embrace with his shakti, Nairatma, 'No Soul', also known as Nairatmya (**ill. 1**). He is often shown with five heads and sixteen arms and his skin is blue. He is most recognizable by the cups that he holds in all sixteen hands, each supporting various ritual objects or images of animals or gods.

Kevajra
(Mongolian)
Kye-ba Rdo-rje
(Tibetan)

Samvara

Samvara, 'Supreme Bliss', represents the bliss that results from tantric meditation. He is most often worshipped in Tibet and Nepal, and in one of his most common forms, Chakrasamvara, 'Wheel of Supreme Bliss', is closely associated with the Kagyu order of Tibetan Buddhism. Samvara was also venerated in China, where the chief Tibetan Buddhist in Beijing was believed to have been his incarnation. He is usually represented with five heads of different colours, each wearing crowns of skulls and twelve arms, which hold a vajra and a bell, an elephant skin and other objects. He is most often depicted embracing his shakti, Vajravarahi, who is red and carries a chopper (57) and a skull cup (60). Samvara's left foot crushes a female figure, Kalaratri, 'Night of Time', who represents nirvana, and his left foot crushes the male figure Bhairava, who represents samsara, or the world of illusion. Samvara, an emanation of the Buddha Akshobhya (5), often wears an image of this Buddha in his crown.

Sanbaluo
(Chinese)
Bde-mchog
(Tibetan)

Kalachakra

Kalachakra, 'Wheel of Time', is the deification of the ancient concept of the wheel, or cycle of time. He is worshipped in Tibet, Nepal, and Mongolia. An important yidam, he is always represented in sexual embrace with his shakti, Vishvamata, and has four heads, each with a third eye, and twelve or twenty-four arms. His body is blue and that of his consort is orange. He carries a vajra, a sword and other weapons and ritual objects, and crushes demons or four-armed human figures under his feet (**ill. 3**).

Chag-un Kurde
(Mongolian)
Dus-'khor
(Tibetan)

1 Indra, painted wood, Indonesia, 19th century (left)

2 Brahma, Japan (above)

3 Prthivi, Japan, 17th century (below)

The devas are gods who inhabit the celestial regions of the Buddhist universe, one of the six stages in the cycle of rebirth (70). Many of these gods derive from Hindu, or the earlier Brahmanic pantheons, and are believed to have offered their services to the Buddha as protectors of the Buddhist Law. They possess many of the characteristics of these Indian gods, but they are spiritually inferior and less evolved than the Buddha, a perfected being who has attained release. Although they are superior to human beings, they are also striving for release from the cycle of rebirth.

There are many devas in the Buddhist pantheon, but the group of Twelve Great Devas contains the most commonly worshipped of these gods, and certain Chinese Buddhist texts claimed that all of the many devas can be represented by these twelve. These deities are rarely worshipped alone and are most often represented in mandalas. Of the twelve devas, eight correspond to the eight directions, while the remaining four represent the earth, sky, sun and moon:

(1) Indra (East) is the most powerful of all of the devas, the lord of all the gods of Hinduism and Buddhism. He is most often represented as a bodhisattva sitting in the royal ease position (38) on the back of a white elephant (**ill. 1**).

(2) Agni (Southeast) is the deity of the pre-Hindu sacrificial fire and is usually depicted surrounded by flames.

(3) Yamaraja (South) is one of the Ten Kings of Hell (71) and is the supreme judge of the dead.

(4) Nirrti (Southwest) is king of the ashuras (26) and is often represented as a demonic figure with red skin and wearing armour and carrying a sword or club.

(5) Varuna (West) is the ancient pre-Hindu god of the waters and is often coloured blue or grey-green and shown seated on a turtle or a dragon surrounded by water.

(6) Vayu (Northwest) is the ancient pre-Hindu god of the wind, and is often represented riding a deer among the clouds. He usually wears a vajra in his headdress.

(7) Vaishravana (19) (North) is also chief of the Four Heavenly Kings (18).

(8) Isana (Northeast) represents the wrathful aspect of the Hindu god of destruction, Shiva. He is shown holding the trident of Shiva.

(9) Brahma (Sky) was the supreme deity and the great creator god of Hinduism. He is often depicted with four heads, each wearing a crown. He rides a white goose and carries four books, representing the sacred Hindu texts, the Vedas (**ill. 2**).

(10) Prthivi (Earth) is the god or goddess of the earth and is generally depicted as a bodhisattva standing holding a bowl full of seeds or flowers (**ill. 3**).

(11) Surya (Sun) is the pre-Hindu deity of the sun and is usually depicted as a bodhisattva seated astride a group of horses and surrounded by a solar disc or nimbus.

(12) Chandra is the pre-Hindu deity of the moon. He complements Surya, and is generally shown seated on a lotus leaf supported by three white geese. He wears a crescent moon in his hair and holds a lunar disc in his hand.

Tianshen
   (Chinese)
ch'on *(Korean)*
Ten, Tennin
   (Japanese)
Lha Y-dam
   (Tibetan)
Tegri
   (Mongolian)
Tep, Deb *(Thai)*

1 Prajnaparamita, stone, Khmer, Thailand, 12th century (left)

2 Sarasvati, Japan (above)

3 Marici, Japan (below)

In the Buddhist pantheon, there are various types of female deities. Some are the shakti (25) or female counterparts, representing the active female energies of male Buddhas, bodhisattvas, and deities. Others are feminine incarnations of specific Buddhist concepts. Others still entered Buddhism from the Hindu pantheon.

Prajnaparamita

This goddess is the deification of the *Prajnaparamita Sutra*, or the *Perfection of Wisdom Sutra*, a text which, according to Buddhist legend, was entrusted by the Buddha to the nagas (54) until the time when the faithful were ready to hear it. It was discovered by the Indian monk, Nagarjuna, in the first or second century AD and was disseminated to followers of the Buddhist Law. In Southeast Asia, particularly in Cambodia and Java, she is sometimes considered to be the female counterpart of Avalokiteshvara (8), and appears as a bodhisattva with either one head and two arms or with eleven heads and twenty-two arms (**ill. 1**). In Tibet, she is a yellow or white bodhisattva wearing a crown and jewels. In most depictions, she holds the *Prajnaparamita Sutra*. The goddess, Prajnaparamita, appears not to have existed in India, and was not worshipped in China and is rarely seen in Japan or Korea.

Banruopoluomi
 (Chinese)
Hannya
 (Japanese)
Shes-rab-pha-
 rol-tu-phyn-na
 (Tibetan)
Bilig-un
 Chinadu
 Kichagara
 Kuruk-sen
 (Mongolian)

Sarasvati

Sarasvati is a female Hindu deity, who, from even pre-Hindu times, has been worshipped in India as the goddess of learning, and in particular music and poetry. As such, she is usually recognizable by the *vina*, a lute-like instrument that she plays (**ill. 2**). As a Buddhist goddess, she is rarely represented in China or Tibet, where she appears either sitting playing the vina or in a multi-headed tantric form. In Japan from around the fifteenth century AD, she began to attract a large following as a goddess of good luck, and she later became one of Japan's Seven Lucky Gods (Japanese: Shichifukujin), the only female among a group of male popular deities. Sarasvati is often depicted with her fifteen or sixteen children, representing the various crafts of which she is patron.

Dabiancaitian Nu
 (Chinese)
Benzaiten
 (Japanese)
Dbyangs-chan-
 ma, Ngag-gi
 Lha-mo (Tibetan)
Kele-yin ukin
 Tegri
 (Mongolian)

Marici

Marici, 'Ray of Light', is a deity associated with the dawn, and in Tibet was invoked by lamas every day at sunrise. There, she is worshipped as Vajravarahi, 'Vajra Sow', and is the shakti of Samvara (22). She often has three heads, including one of a boar or a pig, symbolizing delusion. She is worshipped in China as the Queen of the Heavens, and in Japan, she is believed to reside in the Great Bear constellation. She is usually yellow and has three heads and eight or sixteen arms, with which she holds a vajra, a hook, and arrow and other objects. She is usually depicted riding a boar (**ill. 3**).

Molizhi Tiannu
 (Chinese)
Marishi-ten
 (Japanese)
Hod-zer Chan-
 ma (Tibetan)

1 Dakini, gilded bronze, Sino-Tibet, 18th century (right)

2 Mahamayuri, Tibet (above)

3 Bodhisattva and shakti in yab-yum embrace, painting in colours on cloth (detail), Tibet, 18th century (below)

Dakinis

Dakinis, 'Sky Walkers', are female deities who possess supernatural wisdom or power. They belong to Vajrayana Buddhism and are worshipped mainly in Tibet, where they symbolize wisdom. The dakinis are usually depicted in a dancing pose, with a fierce facial expression and often without clothing (**ill. 1**). There are many dakinis, but a group of five in particular correspond to the Five Dhyani Buddhas. Buddhadakini holds a wheel and a magic staff and wears a necklace of skulls, and dances on two people. Vajradakini holds a vajra and a skull cup, carries a magic staff, and crushes a corpse under her foot. Ratnadakini holds a precious jewel, Padmadakini holds a lotus, and Visvadakini holds a double vajra.

Rakshas

The five Rakshas are only worshipped in the Vajrayana tradition in Tibet and Nepal as the feminine forms of the Five Dhyani Buddhas. They are often depicted as bodhisattvas seated on thrones or animals and hold distinguishing attributes in two or more arms. In the north is Mahamayuri, who is associated with Amoghasiddhi (7), but is also a non-wrathful manifestation of Shakyamuni (1). She protects against disasters and snake bites and brings rain. She is usually white and sits on the back of a peacock (**ill. 2**). In the south is Mahapratisara, who protects against bodily harm. She has yellow skin and wears an image of Ratnasambhava (7) in her crown. In the west, corresponding to Amitabha (6), is Mahasitavati, who is red and protects against ferocious animals and poisonous plants. In the East is Maharaksha Mantranusharini, who corresponds to Akshobhya (5). In the centre is Mahasahasrapramardani, who is white with six arms and has an image of Vairochana (4) in her crown. She protects against earthquakes and storms.

Shaktis

Shaktis represent the active energy of the male deities of the Buddhist pantheon, and are most often represented in sexual embrace with their male counterparts (**ill. 3**). The concept of the active female counterpart of a male deity originates in the female consorts of Hindu gods, although in Hinduism the female force is usually passive. They appear frequently in the Vajrayana Buddhist pantheon of Tibet and Nepal as bodhisattvas wearing jewels and a crown and share the attributes of their male counterparts. There are five main shaktis, corresponding to the Five Dhyani Buddhas. In the centre, with Vairochana, is Vajradharishvari, who is white and holds a jewel and a triangle. In the east, with Akshobhya, is Lochana, who is grey and holds vajras placed vertically on lotus flowers. In the south is Mamaki, who corresponds to Ratnasambhava, and holds peacock feathers. In the west, with Amitabha, is Pandara, who is pink and holds blue lotuses. In the north, with Amoghasiddhi, is Tara (9), who is light green and holds double vajras on lotuses.

Mkha'-'gro-ma
(Tibetan)

1 Ashura, Japan (left)

2 Yaksha, Java, Indonesia, 11th century (below left)

3 Apsara, Japan (below right)

Ashuras

The ashuras are divine warring beings who inhabit one of the Buddhist Six Realms of Rebirth (70), the unpleasant Realm of the Ashuras. These beings have their origins in ancient Indian mythology, where they were 'anti-gods' and the enemies of the devas (23), or gods. They are rarely depicted in the art of any Buddhist culture, except in images of the various realms of rebirth, where they are shown fighting with swords, spears and other weapons. Where they are depicted, they are shown as wrathful beings with wild, spiky hair, multiple heads and arms (**ill. 1**). In certain Japanese images of the King of the Ashuras, the figure has three heads, the central one with a pained expression, while the two others appear fierce and angry. He has six arms, the central two joined in prayer, the other four holding the sun, moon, bow and arrows.

Axialuo, Axulun
  (Chinese)
Ashura (Japanese)
Lha-ma-yin
  (Tibetan)
Assuri (Mongolian)

Yakshas

Yakshas have their origins in the pre-Buddhist male deities of ancient India. They were absorbed into the Buddhist pantheon as protectors of the Buddha and the Buddhist Law, and were also considered to be male nature spirits. In regions of Southeast Asia, particularly in Java, they have assumed the role of temple guardians, while in Japan, they appear to have merged with mythical beings of indigenous folklore (**ill. 2**). In general, these semi-divine beings are represented as stocky male figures, usually only wearing a loin cloth and jewelry. They are often depicted with beards and bulging eyes. Occasionally, they are shown wearing crowns and earrings, but in general, they do not have many distinguishing attributes.

Yecha (Chinese)
Yasha (Japanese)
Gnod-shyin
  (Tibetan)
Yak, Nhak (Thai)

Apsaras

Apsaras are celestial beings who attend other deities and appear in Buddhist imagery throughout Asia as decorative details in paintings and temple architecture. They are most often depicted flying through the air or sitting or standing on lotuses or clouds wearing light, flowing garments that appear to be blowing in the wind (**ill. 3**). They often resemble bodhisattvas dancing or playing musical instruments in the presence of a major deity, and in some cases, they hold their hands together in a gesture of prayer (44). They are often present in depictions of Buddhist paradises (72) from Tibet and Japan, creating the celestial music of these glorious Pure Lands. Apsaras are not objects of worship, but are themselves devotees of the Buddha, and often appear to be worshipping the Buddha or other figures. In East Asia, they appear as decorative elements of bronze Buddhist bells and temple lanterns. In Southeast Asian cultures, they appear as bejewelled female dancers, and their images adorn the Buddhist sanctuaries of Thailand, Laos, and Cambodia. Some of the most exquisite representations of these celestial beings are carved into the walls of the Buddhist temples of Angkor (80) in Cambodia.

Tiannu, Feitian
  (Chinese)
Tennin, Hiten
  (Japanese)
Lha'i Bu-mo
  (Tibetan)
Tevoda, Nang-fa
  (Thai)
Tepanom (Khmer)
Tien Nu (Vietnamese)

1 Arhat and attendant, painting on satin, China, c. 1600 (above)

2 Arhat, Panthaka, Japan (top left)

3 Arhat in cave, jade, China, 17th century (centre left)

4 Five hundred arhats on Vulture Peak, Japan, 17th century (left)

Identity

‘Arhat’ is a pre-Buddhist Indian term that refers to one who has understood the truth about reality. In the Southern schools of Buddhism, the arhats are holy men or sages who have realized the Buddhist doctrine and have attained enlightenment, and are thus assured of attaining nirvana at death. An arhat is an ideal figure in the Southern schools, who do not distinguish between an arhat and a Buddha. In the Northern schools, however, they are less important than the bodhisattvas, who seek not only their own enlightenment, but that of all other beings.

It is generally believed that the Buddha entrusted his teachings to sixteen principal arhats and their disciples. Arhats are therefore also protectors and preservers of the Buddhist Law. In the Northern schools of Buddhism, these have become the Sixteen Immortal Arhats: Pindola Bharadvaja, Kanakabhadra, Kanakavasta, Subinda, Nakula, Bhadra, Kalika, Vajraputra, Jivaka, Panthaka, Rahula, Nagasena, Angaja, Vanavasin, Ajita, and Chudapanthaka. All of these arhats came from different backgrounds, and one, Rahula, is said to be the son of the Buddha. They all studied the Buddhist Law and attained enlightenment. Many legends arose around these holy men, attributing to them colourful characters or magical powers. Some texts describe fifty or five hundred arhats who accompanied the Buddha and, like bodhisattvas, promised to postpone their own enlightenment to help others.

Principal Areas of Worship

The arhats are widely worshipped in China, where a group of eighteen, the traditional sixteen plus two Chinese additions, has been venerated since around the tenth century AD. Chinese legends also tell of a group of five hundred arhats living on the sacred Mount Tiantai. Arhats also gained a following in Tibet, where the monks Dharmatala and Huashan were added to the sixteen Indian arhats. In Japan, arhats have been worshipped in groups of sixteen or five hundred since around the twelfth century, in particular by monks of the Obaku Zen sect, which was established in the seventeenth century by Chinese monks fleeing China after the collapse of the Ming dynasty. The arhats are occasionally worshipped as individuals, but they are more often venerated in groups for their collective power.

Representations and Attributes

In paintings, arhats are generally depicted as elderly monks with shaved heads and wearing loose robes (**ill. 1**). They often carry staffs or other attributes which identify the particular figure. Pindola Bharadvaja is usually depicted as an old man with white hair and bushy eyebrows, seated on a rock holding a sceptre or a box of sutras. Bhadra is often accompanied by a tiger, while Panthaka is usually accompanied by a dragon (**ill. 2**). Sculptures of the arhats are also very common in Japan and China, where the holy men are often depicted in caves sitting reading Buddhist texts (**ill. 3**). In certain images of the Buddha preaching his Law on Vulture Peak, the arhats are shown as a crowd of monks surrounding him, listening to his teachings (**ill. 4**).

lohan (*Chinese*)
rakan (*Japanese*)
gnas-brtan
  (*Tibetan*)
batu-aqchi
  (*Mongolian*)

1 Bodhidharma on a reed, embroidered silk, Japan/China, 20th century (left)

2 Bodhidharma carrying courtesan, painting on silk by Ogawa Ritsuo, c. 1740, Japan (above right)

3 Seated Bodhidharma, Japan (below right)

4 Bodhidharma toy, papier maché, Japan, 20th century (below)

Identity

Bodhidharma is believed to have been a Buddhist monk who was born in India and travelled to China in the sixth century AD in order to transmit meditational, or dhyana, Buddhism to the Chinese. According to legend, Bodhidharma crossed the sea on a single reed and arrived in Guangzhou (Canton), around 527 AD. He is believed to have taught meditation to the warrior monks of the Shaolin temple in Henan province as a means of cultivating their internal as well as external strength. This type of Buddhism became known as Chan in China and Zen in Japan, where meditational Buddhism became extremely popular among the samurai warriors around the thirteenth century. Bodhidharma is also said to have spent nine years sitting meditating in the lotus position facing a wall, resulting in the loss of the use of his arms and legs. Another legend tells that he cut off his eyelids in order to stay awake during meditation.

Principal Areas of Worship

Bodhidharma is worshipped mainly in China and Japan as the patriarch of Chan, or Zen, Buddhism. He is also considered by many practitioners of the martial arts to be their patriarch as he taught the cultivation of the inner strength that was necessary for a warrior. In Japan, Bodhidharma, known as Daruma, has both a serious and a comical role. In the former role, this semi-mythical figure is considered a model for those seeking to conquer their physical selves and attain clarity through meditation. Daruma is most commonly seen in his comical form, a small round ball with a face, which acts as a powerful talisman that offers protection and good fortune.

Representations and Attributes

Bodhidharma is represented in many ink paintings by Chan or Zen artists as an old Indian priest with a shaved head and wearing red robes. He is either shown seated in the lotus position (38) in deep meditation (**ill. 3**), or standing on a reed floating on the sea, an image that represents his voyage from India to China (**ill. 1**). He is sometimes shown from the back seated inside a cave meditating facing a wall. Often, only his face and shoulders are depicted with very few brush strokes. He is usually shown with large, bulging eyes with no eyelids and a sullen expression.

Some of the most fascinating representations are found in Japan, where the most popular images of Daruma are papier maché or wooden balls, painted red for good luck. These balls are usually weighted so that when they are toppled, they roll into an upright position again, symbolizing the idea that no one can strike down a person who obeys the Buddhist Law (**ill. 4**). In Japan during the Edo period (1600–1868), Daruma also became closely associated with the courtesans of the Pleasure Quarters of major cities, and is often represented as a lecherous old man standing next to a beautiful young courtesan, suggesting the contrast between inner, spiritual beauty and outer, physical beauty, or perhaps implying that enlightenment can be found in all areas of life (**ill. 2**).

Damo dashi,
  Putidoluo
  (*Chinese*)
Bodai daruma,
  Daruma
  (*Japanese*)
Talma (*Korean*)

1 Padmasambhava with magic staff and vajra, Tibet (left)

2 Padmasambhava (Guru Rinpoche), brass with traces of gilding, Eastern Tibet, 16th century (below)

3 Padmasambhava, painting on silk (detail), Tibet, 18th century (below left)

Identity

Padmasambhava, 'Lotus Born', was an Indian monk who was invited by the Tibetan King Trisong Detsen in the eighth century AD to convert the Tibetans to Buddhism. His teachings, a variety of tantric Buddhist practices, have become central in the practice of the Nyingma order, the oldest of the sects of Tibetan Buddhism. He is also believed to have been a tantric exorcist who tamed the demons of the native, pre-Buddhist religions of Tibet who were obstructing the path of Buddhism there.

According to Buddhist legend, a short time after the death of the Historical Buddha, Shakyamuni, King Uddiyana in northwest India threatened to destroy all of the religions in his kingdom if he could not have a son. The bodhisattva Avalokiteshvara (8) noticed this and expressed his fear for the people of King Uddiyana's kingdom to the compassionate Amitabha (6) Buddha, who emitted from his tongue a meteor that landed in a lotus lake in King Uddiyana's kingdom. A few days later, a giant lotus was discovered in the lake containing a young boy who claimed to be the son of wisdom and compassion. The 'lotus-born' boy was adopted by the king. Later in his life, Padmasambhava left the palace to become a Buddhist monk, attained spiritual enlightenment, and converted many individuals and kingdoms to Buddhism. He is said to have achieved many miracles and discovered the power of longevity. Thus, he was able to travel to Tibet several hundred years later.

Principal Areas of Worship

Padmasambhava is deeply revered in Tibet and Bhutan, where he also taught the Buddhist Law. He is venerated by many Tibetans as the transmitter of Buddhism to Tibet, and is particularly venerated by the Nyingma order of Tibetan Buddhists, many of whom regard him as the 'second Buddha'. To the Tibetans, this great Buddhist adept personifies all the attributes of the Buddha, the bodhisattvas, and all other Buddhist adepts and represents the power of all of the divine benevolence directed toward the Tibetan people.

Representations and Attributes

Padmasambhava has eight main manifestations, but is generally represented as a princely figure, wearing a reddish-brown robe and hat (**ill. 3**). In his right hand he holds a vajra and in his left hand he holds a skull cup full of blood. In the crook of his left arm, he supports a magical staff, the *khatvanga*, an instrument used by exorcists (**ill. 1**). At the apex of this staff are often three heads in varying levels of decay: a freshly severed head representing desire, a shrunken head, representing hate, and a skull, representing ignorance. His is often depicted wearing a crown and a robe decorated with lotuses, two other attributes associated with destroying demons (**ill. 2**). He is often shown with his twenty-five main Tibetan disciples or with his two consorts, the Indian princess, Mandarava, and the Tibetan queen, Yeshes Mtsho-rgyal, both of whom were accomplished adepts. He is also sometimes depicted in his Glorious Copper Mountain Pure Land.

Pad-ma
Hbyung-gnas
(Tibetan)

1 Xuanzang, Japan (above)

2 Xuanzang walking, embroidered silk, Japan, 20th century (right)

3 Atisha, gilded bronze, Tibet 16th or 17th century (below)

Xuanzang

Xuanzang (also spelled Hsuan-tsang) was a Chinese monk who travelled from China to India and back in the seventh century in order to learn the true teachings of the Buddha. Not satisfied with the confusing Chinese translations of Buddhist texts that were available in China, Xuanzang set off with his small entourage in 629 AD to the source of Mahayana Buddhist teachings. Over the course of sixteen years, he and his group of pilgrims travelled 10,000 miles across deserts and glaciers to India. When in India, he studied Mahayana Buddhist teachings and wrote many works including his *Record of Western Religions* for the Tang emperor, Gaozong (ruled 649–683). His writings were read widely and inspired many later Buddhist thinkers in China.

Principal Areas of Worship

Xuanzang is not worshipped as a Buddhist deity, but he has been revered over the centuries as a major figure in the development of Chinese Buddhism. However, a Buddhist reliquary called the Great Goose Pagoda was erected in Xian to house the relics and texts that Xuanzang brought back with him from India, and later, another pagoda was built at the Xingjiao temple to house Xuanzang's own remains.

Representations and Attributes

Xuanzang is most often depicted in the garb of a pilgrim monk with a shaved head, a monk's yellow robes, and straw sandals (**ill. 1**). He usually carries a square backpack full of texts and personal items which also served as a sun shade for the long walk through the desert (**ill. 2**). Representations of Xuanzang often appear in Chinese rubbings from stone steles and paintings depicting this pilgrim were found among the treasures of the Dunhuang Buddhist caves in western China.

Atisha

Atisha, an Indian Buddhist monk who travelled to Tibet in the eleventh century, was one of the foremost figures in the establishment of Buddhism in Tibet. Although Buddhism was already flourishing in Western Tibet when Atisha arrived in 1042, the Indian monk then travelled to Central Tibet and eventually established Buddhism there, with the help of several Tibetan disciples. According to legend, it was the goddess Tara, his own personal protective deity, who persuaded him to travel to Tibet. His disciples founded the Kadam order at the Ratreng Monastery in Central Tibet.

Representations and Attributes

Atisha is not a figure of worship in Tibet but is depicted in paintings and sculptures as either a monk seated with his hands in the gesture of the explanation of the Buddhist Law or as a travelling monk. On his back is a square monk's backpack in which he carried sacred Buddhist texts (**ill. 3**).

1 Kobo Daishi holding vajra and beads, Japan (above)

2 Kobo Daishi temple souvenir print, woodblock print , Japan, 19th century (right)

3 Kobo Daishi as a child, painting on silk, Japan, 18th century (below)

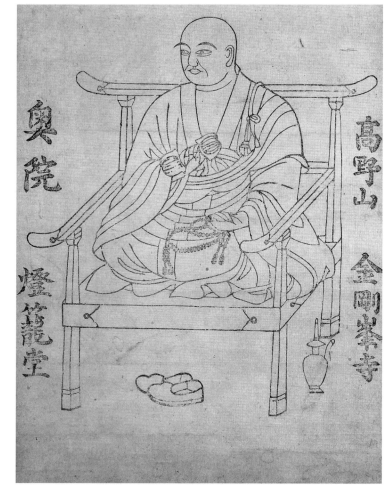

奥院 燈籠堂 高野山 金剛峯寺

The Buddhist priest Kukai (773–835), known posthumously as Kobo Daishi, is the most celebrated priest in Japanese history. The founder of the Shingon, the 'True Word', school of esoteric Buddhism in Japan, he has also been credited with many miraculous acts and innovations including the invention of the Japanese writing system. Kukai had a keen interest in esoteric Buddhism and travelled to China in the first years of the ninth century to study under Hui Guo (746–805), the seventh patriarch of Chinese esoteric Buddhism. He became his successor and took the secret teachings back with him to Japan in 806, establishing his headquarters at Mount Koya near Kyoto in 816.

Although Kukai and Saicho, the founder of Japan's other esoteric school, the Tendai sect, initially exchanged information on esoteric teachings, Kukai took over from his rival as the main religious figure of the ninth century, with members of the Shingon school finding favour with many members of the Imperial court. Shingon Buddhism is similar to the esoteric Buddhist schools of the Himalayan region and involves the use of devices such as mandalas (diagrams, 73), mantras (sacred phrases) and mudras (hand gestures, 41–44) as means of attaining enlightenment.

Principal Areas of Worship

Kobo Daishi is venerated in Japan by practitioners of the Shingon school of esoteric Buddhism, the headquarters of which remain at Mount Koya in Wakayama prefecture. He is also closely associated with the Toji, or Eastern Temple, of Kyoto, where he was appointed abbot in 822. The temple, more formally known as the Monastery for the Salvation of the Emperor and the Protection of the Realm (Japanese: Kyoogokokuji), commands the main entrance to Kyoto, which was once Japan's capital. Kobo Daishi is also associated with a pilgrimage cycle of eighty-eight Shingon temples on the Japanese island of Shikoku.

Representations and Attributes

Kobo Daishi is generally represented as a middle-aged monk seated on a large wooden Chinese-style chair, in a format typical of representations of Chinese and Japanese Buddhist patriarchs (**ill. 1**). In his hands he usually holds vajras (55), which are symbols of esoteric Buddhism. Images of Kobo Daishi are featured on the souvenir prints from the eighty-eight temples of Shikoku that are associated with this monk. Followers traditionally collect a printed image from each temple along the pilgrimage route. Images of Kobo Daishi as a child have also been popular in Shingon Buddhism since the eleventh or twelfth century (**ill. 3**).

1 Eyes of the Buddha, Nepal (above)

2 Elongated earlobes of the Buddha, stone, Ayudhaya, Thailand, 15th century (left)

3 Wrathful face of Bhairava, bronze, Tibet, 18th century (below)

For centuries, Buddhist artists have followed strict rules for the depiction of Buddhas, bodhisattvas, and deities to ensure that the figural representations of these beings possess maximum spiritual power. At an early date, instructions were written down in ancient Indian Hindu and Buddhist painting manuals to enable artists to depict each figure with specific body proportions and characteristics, often corresponding with a form borrowed from nature. These rules followed Buddhism across Asia, although different regions incorporated their own artistic styles into their imagery. The faces of figures of worship were particularly important, since worshippers have traditionally made the strongest connection with this part of the image.

Eyes

In Buddhist imagery, as in that of most traditions, the most important detail of the face is the eyes. Images of the Buddha have traditionally been depicted with eyes half closed as if in meditation. However, the eyes do not appear as simple slits, but are given the shape of lotus petals (**ill. 1**), in keeping with more ancient painting instructions. The eyebrows, in turn are supposed to resemble two bows arching elegantly over the eyes. In many images of the Buddha, particularly Thai images from the Sukhothai period in the thirteenth and fourteenth centuries, the eyebrows generally continue inwards to form the shape of the nose of the Buddha. In images of bodhisattvas, the eyes and eyebrows are given similar treatment to illustrate the serene and compassionate nature of these beings. Wrathful manifestations of these and other beings, however, are depicted with large, round, bulging eyes to denote their aggressive and passionate natures. Guardian figures have large, bulging eyes to scare away the enemies of Buddhism.

Ears

Buddhas and bodhisattvas are often shown with abnormally long earlobes, said to represent their extraordinary wisdom and spiritual advancement (**ill. 2**). It has been suggested that the long earlobes are a sign of royalty, since Indian princes traditionally wore heavy earrings made of gold and precious jewels that stretched their earlobes. In East Asia, long earlobes have traditionally been associated with long life and appear on figures of worship in various religions there, including Buddhism.

Mouths

Buddhas and bodhisattvas are usually depicted with their mouths closed, and in many cases, they wear the hint of a smile, suggesting that they have understood the truth about life. The gentle smile they wear also invites worshippers to have faith in the teachings of the Buddha. Wrathful deities, on the other hand, are typically depicted with open mouths and fangs that enhance their fearsome aspect (**ill. 3**). In the case of pairs of temple gate guardians (20), one of the pair holds his mouth open, saying 'A', while the mouth of the other is closed, uttering 'Um'. The two sounds joined form the mystic syllable, 'Om', which represents the entirety of the cosmos.

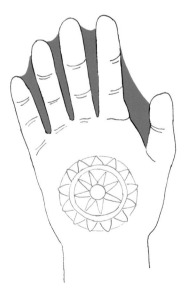

1 Wheels on the soles of the Buddha's feet (below)

2 The Buddha's webbed hands (left)

3 The urna between the eyes and the ushnisha on Buddha's head, Tibetan silk appliqué thangka, 20th century (above)

lakshana

(Sanskrit)

According to pre-Buddhist Indian tradition, there are thirty-two physical markings, or lakshanas, that characterize a great man. These markings appear because of meritorious acts in his previous lives. In the legend of the Historical Buddha, the great sage, Ashita, visited Siddhartha soon after he was born and identified the thirty-two signs on the boy's body. He predicted that he would grow up to be either a great king or a great spiritual teacher. Many of the distinguishing marks derive from animals, plants and other natural forms. Some can be identified in paintings and sculptures of the Historical Buddha, Shakyamuni. According to an ancient Indian text entitled the *Lakshana Sutra*, the marks are as follows:

(1) His feet have a level tread.

(2) There are wheels on the soles of his feet (**ill. 1**).

(3) He has projecting heels.

(4) He has long fingers and toes.

(5) His feet are soft and tender.

(6) His hands and feet are webbed (**ill. 2**).

(7) His ankles are like rounded shells.

(8) His legs are like an antelope's.

(9) His arms are so long that he can touch his knees with his hands without bending.

(10) His male organs are concealed within a sheath.

(11) His complexion is golden.

(12) His skin is so delicate that no dust adheres to his body.

(13) The down on his skin grows in single hairs, one to each pore.

(14) The down is blue-black and turns upwards in little rings curling to the right.

(15) His frame is divinely straight.

(16) His body has seven convex surfaces.

(17) The front half of his body is like a lion's.

(18) There is no furrow between his shoulders.

(19) His proportions have the symmetry of a banyan tree.

(20) His bust is equally rounded.

(21) His taste is supremely acute.

(22) His jaws are like a lion's.

(23) He has forty teeth.

(24) He has regular teeth.

(25) He has continuous teeth.

(26) His eye teeth are very lustrous.

(27) His tongue is long.

(28) He has a divine voice, like the karavika bird's.

(29) His eyes are intensely blue.

(30) His eyelashes are like a cow's.

(31) Between his eyebrows is a hairy mole (urna), white and soft like cotton down (**ill. 3**).

(32) His head is like a royal turban, with a bump in the middle (ushnisha) (**ill. 3**).

1 Crowned bodhisattva, Tibet (above left)

2 Head of the Buddha, bronze, Thailand, 16th century (above right)

3 Bodhisattva with raised hair style, stone, China, early 13th century (above)

4 Head of the Buddha, stucco, Gandhara, 3rd or 4th century (left)

Symbolism and Function

Buddhas, bodhisattvas, and other deities are usually depicted with a specific hairstyle, crown or headdress that provides some indication of their status and role. For example, a Buddha is usually shown with short hair and a protrusion on his head, while a bodhisattva may have long hair tied up in an elegant chignon. The more elaborate hairstyles and headdresses mostly originate in the iconography of Hindu and pre-Hindu Indian art, where they often indicated the royal status of humans and gods. However, in Buddhist imagery, they are not used to indicate material wealth or power as much as the spiritually advanced nature of the beings. These hairstyles, crowns, and headdresses vary in the different Buddhist cultures of Asia, where they have taken on regional characteristics, reflecting local styles and aesthetics.

Representations

The most well known hairstyle in Buddhist art is perhaps that of the Buddha (or various Buddhas of the Northern schools), who is generally depicted with a protrusion on the top of his head and tightly curling hair. The protrusion, or ushnisha, may have originated in a bun hairstyle once worn by the Buddha and other royal personages. However, it is generally considered to be a sign of the Buddha's great wisdom and enlightened state. In some of the earliest images of the Buddha, produced in the first centuries AD in the Gandharan region northwest of India, the Buddha was depicted with wavy hair that originated in Western sculpture of the Greco-Roman tradition (**ill. 4**). In Southeast and East Asian images of the Buddha, the hair has generally been rendered with small, tight curls resembling snail shells. In many Thai and Sri Lankan images, the Buddha's head is crowned with a flame ushnisha that rises upwards into a dramatic point (**ill. 2**).

Bodhisattvas are often depicted with long hair piled up and tied in elegant topknots on top of their heads. Their long hair, worn in a sophisticated style, indicates their continued attachment to and presence in this world (**ill. 3**). Monks, arhats, and other spiritual leaders are generally depicted with shaved heads, an indication of their renunciation of the material world and their devotion to the spiritual life.

Crowns are generally only worn by Buddhist figures of the Mahayana and Vajrayana pantheons and clearly indicate the high status of the wearer. In the imagery of the esoteric schools, in the Himalayas and Japan, Buddhas and bodhisattvas are often represented wearing crowns and jewelry, particularly when depicted in mandalas or paradise scenes, an indication of their high status in the Buddhist pantheon and of their spiritual advancement (**ill. 1**). Their crowns often contain small images of the higher beings with whom they are closely associated. For example, Avalokiteshvara's (8) crown holds an image of the Buddha Amitabha (6), for whom this bodhisattva is an attendant. The wrathful being, Yamantaka (16) often wears an image of the bodhisattva Manjushri (12) in his crown, since he is a wrathful emanation of this bodhisattva. Many wrathful beings wear crowns of skulls which signify their power to conquer evil forces.

1 Crown and jewelry of Green Tara, Tibetan silk appliqué, 20th century (left)

2 Necklace of skulls, Tibet (below left)

3 Temple Guardians, Wat Phra Kaew, Bangkok, Thailand (below right)

Symbolism and Function

In both the Northern and Southern schools of Buddhism, the Historical Buddha (1) is generally portrayed in the simple robes of a monk, with no jewelry or other adornments. This plain, austere appearance signifies his lack of attachment to the material world and his transcendence of this world into a state of enlightenment, or nirvana. Holy men, or arhats (27), are also depicted as monks in simple robes to denote their enlightened state.

Prior to his enlightenment, however, the Buddha Shakyamuni was a prince of a small kingdom, and as such, wore precious jewels, a crown and luxurious silk robes. At this time, since he was destined to become a Buddha, he was still a bodhisattva, a being on the verge of enlightenment. This explains why many images of bodhisattvas are traditionally adorned with jewelry, flowing robes and other decorations, signifying their continued presence in this world as saint-like beings who assist followers of Buddhism towards enlightenment. In the esoteric schools of Buddhism, however, images of the Buddhas are often wear jewelry, crowns, and other adornments and closely resemble bodhisattvas. The jewelry and adornments tend to reflect the styles and aesthetics of the various cultures in which these images were produced.

Representations

Bodhisattvas often wear necklaces and bracelets made of precious jewels to indicate their princely status. Their chests are often bare, and the necklaces hang down, often in several layers, almost covering the chest. On the bodhisattvas' upper and lower arms are often jewelled bracelets, and their elongated earlobes are often adorned with heavy earrings (**ill. 1**). In sculptural representations, the jewelry is often made separately from the rest of the image and placed onto the finished image. In many Himalayan sculptures, the necklaces are inlaid with semi-precious stones such as turquoise and coral. Images of wrathful deities also wear necklaces, bracelets, and other jewelry, but more noticeably, they often wear garlands made of human skulls, representing their triumph over evil forces (**ill. 2**).

While Buddhas are generally depicted in simple monks' robes, bodhisattvas are often depicted in elegant robes that cling to their supple bodies, with sashes and ribbons that flow gracefully around them. In many Indian and Himalayan images, the bodhisattva is shown wearing an Indian dhoti-like loin cloth that wraps around the lower half of the body. The dhoti is often decorated with elaborate patterns and fastened at the front with a decorative knot.

Despite the Buddhist's abhorrence of killing animals, certain bodhisattvas and other figures are depicted wearing animal skins. For example, Maitreya is sometimes depicted with an antelope skin draped over one shoulder. In addition, many images of arhats show the holy men wearing the skins of tigers and other wild animals. Wrathful deities, including demons and temple guardians, are also occasionally depicted in animal skins, but more often, they wear armour and helmets, often heavily decorated, to denote their fearsome characters (**ill. 3**).

1 Buddha seated on a double-lotus throne, gilded bronze, Tibet, 18th century (above)

2 Acalanatha seated on a rocky throne, embroidered silk, Japan/China, 20th century (right)

3 Head and body aureole, Japan (below)

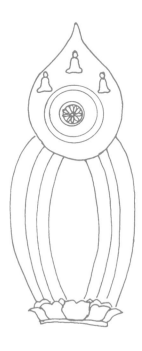

Thrones and Stands

Symbolism and Function

The thrones and stands that the various Buddhas, bodhisattvas, and deities sit on are significant elements of Buddhist iconography and originally appeared in Buddhist art around the second century AD, shortly after the first figural representations of Buddhas and bodhisattvas. They often indicate the character of the being who is seated on them. For example, the Historical Buddha (1) is often seated on a throne decorated with deer representing the Deer Park where he gave his first sermon, or with lions representing the Buddhist Law.

The highest beings in the Buddhist pantheon sit or stand on a lotus throne, since the lotus flower (48) indicates the divine birth and the purity of the being on it. These thrones are sometimes mounted on the backs of lions and other animals (53), who symbolize a particular aspect of the deity's character or function. For example, the bodhisattva, Manjushri (12), who represents the wisdom of the teachings of the Buddha, sits on the back of a lion who represents the power of the Buddha's Law. Lesser deities are often shown sitting or standing on square, rectangular, or diamond-shaped stands or platforms.

Representations

Of all the thrones, the most commonly depicted is the lotus throne, which consists of a disk resting on a lotus flower that has two or more rows of petals. Usually the petals in the lower row point downward, and the upper row point towards the deity (**ill. 1**). In some images of standing Buddhas or bodhisattvas, each foot is shown standing on a separate lotus pedestal. Lesser deities in the Buddhist pantheon do not sit on lotus thrones, but instead sit or stand on platforms that may be carved or painted to resemble rocks, symbolizing the deity's strength and stability, as in images of one of the Five Kings of Mystical Knowledge, Acalanatha, 'The Immovable One', who is generally depicted sitting or standing on a rocky throne, indicating the firmness of his character (**ill. 2**).

Aureoles

Buddhas, bodhisattvas, and other deities are often surrounded by aureoles, or haloes, that indicate their divine nature. These aureoles, or mandorlas, range from simple discs around the deity's head to more complex aureoles containing smaller Buddhist figures, celestial beings, or flaming pearls, and surrounding both the head and the body. In general, an elaborate aureole signifies a higher being, usually a Buddha or a bodhisattva. Flaming aureoles generally surround wrathful deities. Head aureoles are usually circular or slightly pointed upwards in the form of a precious jewel. Body aureoles are commonly either rounded or boat-shaped with a point at the top (**ill. 3**; see also p. 102, ill. 1). Both body and head aureoles are rendered in gold in painting and sculpture to represent the divine light emanating from the being.

pitha (Sanskrit)
zuo (Chinese)
za (Japanese)

chakra (Sanskrit)
kohai (Japanese)

1 Standing Amitabha Buddha, wood, Japan, 18th–19th century (left)

2 Standing bodhisattva, silver with gilt and precious stones, Tibet, 14th century (below)

3 Walking Buddha, Thailand, 16th century (right)

Many Buddhas, bodhisattvas, and deities are depicted either standing or striking a dynamic pose. These positions generally relate to the character and role of the deity, the more enlightened Buddhas and bodhisattvas adopting more static poses that suggest their transcendence of this world, while guardian figures and wrathful deities strike vigorous poses to denote their vibrant presence in this realm.

Standing Postures

Images of certain Buddhas, particularly the Historical Buddha, Shakyamuni (1), and Amitabha (6) Buddha, are often depicted standing facing forward on a lotus pedestal with legs slightly parted. These Buddhas, enlightened beings who are no longer in this world, generally hold their hands in the gestures of fearlessness (41) and possess an air of meditative calm (**ill. 1**). In images of the Historical Buddha as an infant, the child Buddha is shown standing with his right arm pointing to the sky and his left hand pointing to the earth, declaring that he was the only being worthy of veneration in Heaven and on Earth (see p. 26, ill. 3).

Bodhisattvas and other deities may also be shown standing facing forward, but they are often depicted swaying slightly, in the triple-bend, or tribhanga, pose, that originated in the pre-Buddhist sculptures of India. In these representations, the figure's weight usually rests on one leg and the other leg is placed slightly forward in a very sensual pose that denotes the being's continued presence in our realm (**ill. 2**).

In images of guardian figures and wrathful deities, the triple-bend pose is more pronounced, and the deities raise their hands in rather threatening gestures (see p. 68). Guardian figures also brandish weapons or vajras (55) in their hands and appear poised to attack anyone threatening the faith. Certain wrathful deities strike poses that resemble a wild dance, with the left foot on the ground and the right foot raised in the air. In some cases, the deity tramples a dwarf or other being that represents ignorance or evil. Such depictions derive from pre-Buddhist Indian images of Shiva, Lord of the Dance, who dances wildly while trampling the dwarf of ignorance.

Walking Postures

In images of the Buddha from Thailand, Laos, and Vietnam, the Buddha is sometimes shown in a walking pose that is unique to these cultures and is believed to have originated in Thailand during the Sukhothai (79) period, around the thirteenth century (**ill. 3**).This posture is also known as the 'placing of the Buddha's footprint' (46). These Buddhas standing with their weight on one foot and the other foot slightly raised behind the body. They often have their right hand raised in the fearlessness gesture (41) and the left hand hanging by the side of the body. Because the figure is walking forward, the body appears to be swaying slightly to one side. This walking pose is the most dynamic representation of the Historical Buddha in the Southern Theravada Buddhist tradition and is not found in the Northern Buddhist traditions.

1 Lotus position, Japan (above left)

2 Buddha in lotus position, stone, c. 800, Borobodur, Java (left)

3 Buddha seated in European position, bronze, China, 8th century (above)

4 Avalokiteshvara in royal ease position, gilt bronze, India, c. 1150 (below)

Lotus Position (Sanskrit: Padmasana)

Most seated Buddhist figures are depicted in the lotus position. There are several variations: in the full lotus position, the legs are folded at the knees and the feet are crossed, soles upwards (**ill. 1, 2**). In images of the Historical Buddha (1), this posture may reveal wheels on the soles of his feet. In the half-lotus position one or both feet are hidden beneath the Buddha's robe, suggesting the esoteric nature of the Buddha.

European/Chinese Posture (Sanskrit: Bhadrasana)

This posture is seen in sculptures from all Buddhist cultures, but is usually reserved for figures of the Buddha. In this posture, the Buddha, usually the Historical Buddha, but sometimes Maitreya (3), is seated on a throne with legs pendant, and occasionally crossed at the ankles (**ill. 3**). In some examples, the feet rest on a small stool, raising the knees. This is a very old sitting position, first seen in the stone sculptures of Gandharan region, located in northwest India, Pakistan and Afghanistan, where Greco-Roman artistic influence was strong. It is also found in the sculptures and painting of Southeast Asia, the Himalayan region, and in East Asia.

Relaxation Posture (Sanskrit: Lalitasana, Rajalilasana)

This posture is somewhere between the lotus position and the European position. The Buddha or bodhisattva sits on a throne with one leg folded and the other pendant, to one side or in the centre. This position is also common in images of bodhisattvas and deities shown on the backs of support animals, such as Manjushri (12) on the back of a lion. A variant of this posture is rajalilasana, or 'King Royal Ease Position', in which one leg is folded horizontally and the other is bent vertically, in a position that is only used for Buddhas and bodhisattvas and other regal personages (**ill. 4**).

Contemplation Posture (Sanskrit: Maitreyasana)

Maitreya, the Buddha of the Future, is often shown seated on a throne with his left leg pendant and his right leg folded over his left knee. His right elbow leans on his right knee and the fingers of his right hand lightly touch his right cheek. This posture suggests that the Future Buddha is contemplating the right moment to descend from his heaven to save our world. It is most commonly seen in Korean and early Japanese depictions of Maitreya (see p. 32, ill. 3).

Kneeling Posture

Figures shown kneeling are generally lesser deities showing their devotion towards more enlightened beings. In Japan, Amitabha (6) is often shown flanked by the bodhisattvas Avalokiteshvara (8) and Mahasthamaprapta who kneel with their hands in the gesture of prayer (44). In the lower corners of some Buddhist paintings, the donors who have commissioned the paintings are shown kneeling in prayer, demonstrating their devotion to the Buddha or bodhisattva depicted.

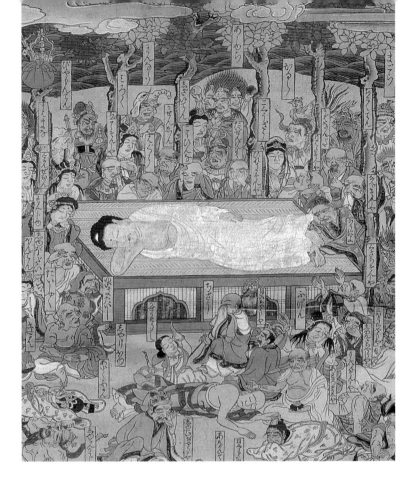

1 Dying Buddha and his disciple Ananda, stone, Polonnaruwa, Sri Lanka, 12th century (below)

2 Death Scene of the Buddha, hand-coloured woodblock print (detail), Japan, 18th century (right)

Symbolism and Function

The lying position is only seen in images of Shakyamuni (1) and it represents the Buddha at his mortal passing and his final release from the cycle of rebirth. It is the fourth of the principal postures of the Buddha, representing the four main events in his life. Although the Buddha attained enlightenment, or nirvana, while meditating beneath a bodhi, or pipal tree (51), this enlightenment was not total. Only when he died at the age of eighty-one was he able to shed his corporeal form and enter into nirvana. Therefore, images of him at his death are symbolic of his final release, or parinirvana, and the lying position is known as parinirvanasana.

Representations

Images of the Buddha in parinirvanasana are particularly prevalent in Sri Lanka and Southeast Asia, where the Southern schools of Buddhism favour representations of this and the other events in the life of the Historical Buddha. In Sri Lanka and Southeast Asian countries such as Thailand and Burma, massive sculptural depictions of reclining Buddhas are relatively common, and are usually outside the main temple buildings. At Polonnaruwa (77) in Sri Lanka, a colossal stone sculpture showing the Buddha at the point of death accompanied by his favourite disciple, Ananda, has been carved out of a rock face (**ill. 1**). Such huge stone images originated in India, where examples from the sixth century can still be found in the Buddhist caves at Ajanta (76).

In both paintings and sculptures, the Buddha is shown lying on his right side wearing the robes of a monk. Usually his right hand supports his head and his left hand rests on his left hip. His face is usually very serene, and his eyes can be depicted both open and closed. In some images, particularly those from Southeast Asia, he is actually shown smiling. The image of the dying Buddha is not supposed to evoke sadness as much as a feeling that all beings have the potential to become enlightened and attain release from the cycle of rebirth.

In China and Japan in particular, there are many paintings depicting the death scene of Shakyamuni and his passage from mortality to nirvana. He is depicted on his death bed in a grove of sala trees (51) in Kushinagara on a cloudy night with a full moon. Shakyamuni lies on his right side facing north, with his right hand supporting his head. He is surrounded by weeping followers from all realms – human beings, gods, guardian kings, demons, bodhisattvas, animals, and insects (**ill. 2**). Even his mother, Queen Maya, arrives from Heaven with a priest and two servants on a cloud at the top right of the paintings. Of all the figures present, the only figure who does not lament his passing is his chief disciple, Ananda, who is depicted sleeping peacefully, as he has understood that the physical death is merely a transition to a transcendental state. Such paintings are displayed at homes and temples on the anniversary of the Buddha's death, celebrated on the fifteenth day of the second lunar month.

parinirvanasana
 (Sanskrit)
daniepan *(Chinese)*
nehanzo *(Japanese)*

1 Bodhisattva embracing consort, wood with polychrome and gilding, China, 15th century (right)

2 Bodhisattva Vajrasattva and consort in yab-yum embrace , Tibet (above)

Symbolism and Function

In Buddhist philosophy, the two most important forces in the universe are wisdom (Sanskrit: prajna) and compassion (Sanskrit: karuna). Both must be present for harmony to exist in the universe and for enlightenment to be possible. In visual terms, particularly in the Buddhist imagery of Tibet and Nepal, compassion is represented by a male being, a Buddha, bodhisattva, or deity, while wisdom is represented by a female deity, shown as his consort. These two forces are related to the pre-Buddhist Indian concept of *shiva* and *shakti*, the former being the male universal force and the latter the female. In Hinduism, the male force is active and the female passive; this is reversed in the Buddhist tradition. In Himalayan Buddhism, each of the male Buddhas and bodhisattvas has a specific female counterpart, for example, Vajrapani (14) and his female consort, Sujata.

In Himalayan Buddhist imagery, the unity of the male and the female, and hence the unity of wisdom and compassion, is usually represented by two deities locked in sexual embrace. Such images, most commonly known by their Tibetan name, yab-yum, or 'father-mother' images, are not erotic images. Instead, they personify the concept that wisdom and compassion are perfect complements, and the two must be united for enlightenment to be possible. The embrace signifies this union.

Representations

Most yab-yum paintings and sculptures are from Tibet or Nepal, although some Chinese and Southeast Asian examples, heavily influenced by Tibetan art, also exist. When the figures are seated, the male deity is seated on a throne in the lotus position or with one leg hanging outside the throne. His female partner sits facing him with her legs wrapped around his back (**ill. 1**). In earlier images from India and some Khmer pieces, the female deity is simply shown seated on the knee of the male deity. The 'tight embrace pose' in which the female deity is completely wrapped around her partner is most often seen in figures from Tibet and Nepal (**ill. 2**). When the figures are standing, the female figure, who has her legs wrapped around her partner, is often completely lifted off the ground (see p. 56, ill. 3). In paintings and sculptures of wrathful deities embracing their partners, the union is particularly elaborate, as both of the deities are often depicted with several heads and numerous arms and legs.

Images of male and female deities embracing are not present in East Asian esoteric Buddhist art. However, in the Shingon imagery of Japan, the concept of this union is expressed colourfully through the union of the Mandalas of the Two Worlds (73), namely the male Diamond World and the female Womb World. At the centre of the Diamond World, the Cosmic Buddha, Vairochana (4), further enforces this union with the hand gesture known as the fist of wisdom (44), in which the erect finger of the left hand, representing the male universal force, or compassion, is enclosed by the right fist, representing the female universal force, or wisdom. The same concept is also given form in the vajraghanta, a ritual object that combines the vajra (55), the male force, and the bell (58), the female force.

1 Standing Buddha making the
fearlessness mudra, bronze, India,
12th century (above left)

2 Seated Buddha making gift giving
gesture, bronze, Swat Valley,
Pakistan, 8th century (below left)

3 Combination of fearlessness and
gift-giving mudras (above)

abhaya mudra *(Sanskrit)*
shiwuwei Yin *(Chinese)*
semui-in *(Japanese)*
simuoe-in *(Korean)*

The abhaya, or 'fearlessness' gesture, is one of the most commonly used mudras (hand gestures) in the art of both the Northern and Southern Buddhist traditions and represents benevolence and the absence of fear. The gesture confers onto others the same freedom from fear, so can also mean 'fear not'. Made only by Buddhas and bodhisattvas, the gesture is made with the right hand raised to shoulder height, with the arm bent and the palm facing outward. The gesture is an old one, originally a sign of friendship and peace, since the hand raised is empty of weapons. The gesture indicates the fearlessness, and hence the spiritual power of the Buddha or bodhisattva making it. According to Buddhist legend, when the Historical Buddha was being attacked by an angry elephant, he simply held up his hand in the fearlessness gesture and calmed the raging beast.

The abhaya mudra is nearly always used in images of standing Buddhas and bodhisattvas, and is also common in seated forms. In the Southern tradition of Buddhism, images of the standing Buddha often hold the right hand in abhaya, while the left hand hangs loosely at the side of the body (**ill. 1**). In Thailand and Laos, sculptures of the Walking Buddha, which are unique to this region, often hold the right hand in abhaya (see also p. 102, ill. 3). In some Southeast Asian images of the Buddha, both hands are held in abhaya mudra. The gesture is often made in combination with another mudra made by the left hand, usually the varada mudra, or gift giving gesture (**ill. 3**)

varada mudra
 (Sanskrit)
shiyuan yin *(Chinese)*
yogan-in *(Japanese)*
siwon-in, segan-in,
 seyo-in *(Korean)*

Varada, 'gift giving' or 'wish granting', is another gesture made mostly by Buddhas and bodhisattvas, generally with the left hand but occasionally with the right. In standing images, the figure stands upright with the left hand hanging at the side of the body with the palm open and facing forward. In seated images, the arm is bent and rests on the knee with the open palm facing upwards (**ill. 2**). The gesture represents the wish of the Buddha or bodhisattva to devote itself to human salvation, and symbolizes charity, compassion, and the fulfilment of wishes. In one sutra, Avalokiteshvara (8), the bodhisattva of compassion, visited the kingdom of the dead, and on reaching the worst of the hells, stood with one hand in varada mudra. From this hand flowed the water of life which nourished and soothed the tormented souls in this hell.

This mudra is most often made by Buddhas or compassionate bodhisattvas, both seated and standing. This gesture is often used in combination with the fearlessness mudra (**ill. 3**), although the second hand often holds the main attribute of the Buddha or bodhisattva. For example, the female bodhisattva Tara (9) often holds her right hand in the gift-giving mudra and grasps a lotus in her left hand.

1 Explanation gesture using both hands (below left)

2 Bodhisattva forming the explanation gesture, silver, Tibet, fourteenth century (above)

3 The gesture of the Turning of the Wheel of the Law (above right)

4 Preaching Buddha, bronze with black pigment, India, Kashmir, or Pakistan, Gilgit, 794 AD (right)

The vitarka, or 'explanation' mudra, is one that is closely associated with the Historical Buddha, Shakyamuni (1), and one of the phases of his preaching, namely the discussion of the dharma, or Buddhist Law. The gesture is believed to convince listeners of the truth of the dharma and lead them to conversion. The mudra is made by forming the fearlessness and gift giving mudras with both hands and allowing the thumb and forefingers of each hand to touch (**ill. 1**). The joining of the thumb and the forefinger forms a circle that represents perfection, or enlightenment. The gesture may also be made with only one hand, allowing the figure to hold an attribute in the other hand (**ill. 2**).

This gesture is mostly used by Buddhas and bodhisattvas both standing and seated. In some seated figures of the Medicine Buddha, Bhaishajyaguru (2), the left hand is in vitarka mudra and also holds a medicine jar. There are variants of this mudra in which the thumb touches fingers other than the forefinger. In Tibetan images of Tara (9) and other bodhisattvas, the thumb is joined with any one of the other fingers. A variant of this mudra is used by deities embracing in the yab-yum position (40), in which the hands in vitarka mudra are crossed at the wrists with the palms facing the deity's breast. In mandalas (73) and other esoteric Buddhist paintings, certain Buddhas are shown with their hands in a variant of vitarka mudra, the right hand in varada and the left clutching a piece of his robe.

vitarka mudra
(Sanskrit)
anwei yin *(Chinese)*
seppo-in, an-i-in
(Japanese)

Gesture of the Turning of the Wheel of the Law 42

Dharmachakra Pravartana mudra, the 'Mudra of the Turning of the Wheel of the Law', represents the first explanation of the dharma by the Historical Buddha. The gesture is made by holding both hands in vitarka mudra, namely with the thumb and forefingers touching or almost touching. Both hands are held close to the chest, with the right palm facing forward and the left either facing upward or turned toward the chest and the separated fingers of the two hands nearly touching (**ill. 3**). The gesture symbolizes one of the key moments in the life of the Historical Buddha, the first sermon that he delivered after achieving enlightenment, in the Deer Park in Sarnath. At this sermon, he explained his philosophy, later known as the Law, or dharma, to a group of listeners. This sermon is believed to have set the figural wheel of his teachings in motion and therefore marked the true beginning of Buddhism as a faith.

Because of its close association with the life and teachings of the Historical Buddha, this gesture is reserved for images of Shakyamuni (**ill. 4**), or occasionally of Maitreya (3), the Buddha of the Future. In some images, wheels are visible on the palms of the Buddha's hands, reinforcing the meaning of the hand gesture. Wheels may also be depicted on the Buddha's feet and on the sides of the throne on which the Buddha is seated.

dharmachakra
  mudra *(Sanskrit)*
juanfalun yin
  (Chinese)
tenborin-in,
  chikichi-jo,
  hoshin-seppo-in
  (Japanese)
chonpobyun-in
  (Korean)

1 Earth-touching gesture (below centre)

2 Seated Buddha making the earth-touching gesture, stone, Ayudhaya, Thailand, 15th century (above)

3 Meditation gesture (below right)

4 Seated Buddha with left hand in meditation gesture, stone, Ayudhaya, Thailand, 15th century (left)

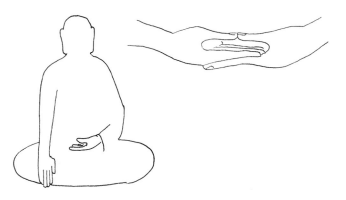

Bhumisparsha mudra, 'the gesture of touching the earth', represents an important moment in the life of the Historical Buddha, Shakyamuni (1) when the Buddha called upon the earth to witness his unshakeable faith and resolve. In this gesture, the Buddha is shown seated in the lotus position (38) with his right hand reaching down over the right knee to touch the ground (**ill. 1**). The left hand usually remains on the lap in meditation mudra (see below).

There are several versions of the legend of how the Buddha came to call upon the earth as witness, but it is generally believed that as the Buddha approached enlightenment, the evil King Mara sent armies of wicked demons and numerous beautiful women to distract the Buddha from his goal of attaining enlightenment. The Buddha was not stirred from his intense meditation, and took the earth as witness of this achievement. Moments later, he attained spiritual enlightenment.

As this mudra is closely associated with the story of the Shakyamuni, it is generally only seen in paintings and sculptures of this particular Buddha (**ill. 2**). However, the transcendental Buddha Akshobhya (5), one of the Five Dhyani Buddhas, also assumes this gesture, as he represents the enlightenment of the Buddha. In Korea, the seated stone Buddha at the cave temple of Sokkuram (86) is considered by some scholars to be a representation of Amitabha (6), although it is represented with this mudra.

bhumisparsha mudra
  (*Sanskrit*)
chudi yin (*Chinese*)
sokuchi-in (*Japanese*)
ch'oji-in (*Korean*)

Gesture of Meditation 43

The dhyana, or 'meditation' mudra, represents the attainment of spiritual perfection or enlightenment and is reserved for Buddhas, in particular Amitabha Buddha. The Buddha sits in the lotus position with both hands at the level of the belly. The right hand rests on the left, with palms facing upwards, the fingers are extended, and the tips of the thumbs touch to form a slightly flattened triangle (**ill. 3**). This is an ancient meditation position used by yogis long before the time of the Historical Buddha during their meditation and concentration exercizes. It was adopted by the Historical Buddha when meditating under the pipal tree before attaining enlightenment and is sometimes used in combination with the earth-touching mudra mentioned above (**ills. 1, 2, 4**). The triangle formed by the fingers represents perfect physical and spiritual balance and symbolizes the Three Jewels (triratna) of Buddhism: the Buddha, his teachings, and the religious community. It is also believed by esoteric schools to symbolize the spiritual fire that consumes all impurities.

dhyana mudra,
  samadhi mudra
  (*Sanskrit*)
ding yin (*Chinese*)
jo-in, jokai Jo-in
  (*Japanese*)
ch'ong-in (*Korean*)

This mudra is most closely associated with Amitabha, the Buddha of Infinite Light, who is often shown seated in meditation with his hands in a variant form of dhyana mudra, with the forefingers bent to touch the thumbs (see p. 38, ill. 1). This variant and two others (in which the two middle fingers or the two ring fingers touch) are used by worshippers of Amitabha, each variant representing higher, middle, and lower levels of rebirth in Amitabha's Pure Land, or Western Paradise.

1 Gesture of the fist of wisdom (above)

2 Vairochana of the Diamond World making the fist of wisdom gesture, embroidered silk, Japan, 20th century (left)

3 Gesture of prayer (below left)

4 Avalokiteshvara with central pair of hands in prayer, lacquered wood, Vietnam, 19th century (below)

bodhyagri
mudra
(Sanskrit)
zhiquan Yin
(Chinese)
chiken-in
(Japanese)

The mudra known as the 'Fist of Wisdom' or the 'Mudra of the Six Elements' is used predominantly in the esoteric imagery of Japan, China, and Korea, and occasionally in Tibet. Despite its sexual symbolism, it appears not to have been used in India. The esoteric gesture is specific to the Cosmic Buddha Vairochana (4), and is made by enclosing the erect forefinger of the left hand in the right fist, with the right forefinger covering the tip of the left (**ill. 1**). The five fingers of the right hand are said to represent the five elements of the universe: earth, water, air, fire, ether, protecting the sixth element, which represents man, or the Buddha mind. The erect forefinger can also be said to represent knowledge, which is hidden by the world of appearances and illusion. The mudra also has strong sexual symbolism, representing the union of the male and female forces of the universe, and is the equivalent in hand gestures of the yab-yum (40) images depicting the sexual union of the male Buddhist deity and his female counterpart, or shakti (25).

This mudra is most commonly depicted in Japanese esoteric representations of the Cosmic Buddha, Vairochana in the Shingon Buddhist context. According to the teachings of Shingon Buddhism, there are two main forms of the Cosmic Buddha: one who is at the centre of the Diamond World Mandala, and the other who is at the centre of the Womb World Mandala. It is the figure of Vairochana in the former mandala who holds his hands in this dynamic gesture (**ill. 2**). The latter Vairochana has his hands in the more passive meditation gesture (43).

Gesture of Prayer 44

anjali mudra
(Sanskrit)
hezhang yin
(Chinese)
hapjang'in
(Korean)
gassho-in
(Japanese)

The anjali mudra, or prayer gesture, is probably the most instantly recognizable and understandable of all of the mudras, as it is a universal gesture of prayer and veneration. In this mudra, the two hands are joined vertically palm against palm in front of the chest (**ill. 3**). This gesture of veneration is not used by the Historical Buddha or any of the other Buddhas, as they are usually the objects of veneration. However, some bodhisattvas are depicted with hands in prayer. For example, the multi-armed form of Avalokiteshvara (8) folds the central pair of arms in the gesture of prayer, while the outer arms hold symbolic objects such as lotuses (48) and water vessels (59, **ill. 4**). In India and Southeast Asia, this mudra is usually made by the praying figures who accompany figures of the Buddha, often at either side of the Buddha figure. Also, in paintings, praying figures are often shown kneeling in one of the lower corners of the painting, and may represent the donor of the painting.

In esoteric Buddhist imagery, there are variants of this mudra, in which the thumbs cross each other, or the tips of the fingers are interlaced. In these variations, the two hands represent the Mandalas of the Two Worlds, the Womb World and the Diamond World (73). The two hands joined are also believed to represent the union of the world of beings (left hand) and the world of the Buddha (right hand).

1 Parasol, Tibet (above far left)

2 Golden Fishes, Tibet (centre far left)

3 Treasure Vase, Tibet (below far left)

4 Lotus, Tibet (centre above)

5 Conch Shell, Tibet (centre)

6 Endless Knot, Tibet (centre below)

7 Victory banner, Tibet (above)

8 Wheel, Tibet (below)

The Eight Auspicious Symbols (Sanskrit: Ashtamangala) appear on many Buddhist objects, textiles and paintings. When they appear as a group, their powers are multiplied. In certain texts, aspects of the Buddha were compared to these symbols, for example, the Buddha's tongue to an open lotus leaf and his head to a protecting parasol.

1 Parasol (Sanskrit: chattra)

The parasol is a symbol of high rank or royalty, as people of wealth and high rank were protected against rain and strong sunshine with parasols, usually carried by servants. In Buddhism, this symbol of material wealth and power symbolizes spiritual power.

2 Golden Fishes (Sanskrit: suvarnamatsya)

The two golden fish, usually depicted head to head, symbolize fertility, since fish produce many offspring. They are also symbols of salvation from suffering.

3 Treasure Vase (Sanskrit: kalasha)

The treasure vase is a symbol of spiritual abundance. The symbolism probably arises from the idea of storing food and may be related to the universal concept of the inexhaustible vessel. In Buddhism, it represents the fulfilment of spiritual wishes.

4 Lotus (Sanskrit: padma) (48)

The lotus is a symbol of mental purity. In nature, the pure white lotus flower rises up out of muddy water, symbolizing the potential of all beings to attain buddhahood .

5 Conch Shell (Sanskrit: sankha) (58)

The conch shell is used by Hindus and Buddhists in religious rituals or to call together an assembly. It symbolizes the fame of the Buddha's teachings.

6 Endless Knot (Sanskrit: shrivasta)

The infinite knot may have originated as two intertwining snakes, and signifies long life, eternal love and the interconnection of all things. The simple, balanced form, with no beginning and no end, symbolizes the infinite knowledge of the Buddha.

7 Victory Banner (Sanskrit: dhvaja)

The victory banner, which is comprised of a cylinder of cloth resembling a parasol, may have its origins in a military banner. In Buddhist terms, it represents the victory of the Buddha's teachings, the victory of knowledge over ignorance and evil.

8 Wheel (Sanskrit: dharmachakra) (47)

The wheel represents the Wheel of the Law, or the dharma, the teachings of the Buddha, the eight spokes representing the Eightfold path and the perfect circular form symbolizing the completeness and perfection of the Buddha's teachings.

1 Footprints of the Buddha, Bodh Gaya (above)

2 Footprint of the Buddha from a souvenir print, Japan (above left and left)

3 Footprints of the Buddha, Bodh Gaya (left)

Symbolism and Function

The footprints of the Buddha represent the presence of the Historical Buddha (1), Shakyamuni. According to Buddhist legend, shortly before the Historical Buddha died and attained his final nirvana, he went to Kushinara and stood upon a stone with his face to the south. He is said to have left an impression of his feet on the stone as a souvenir to posterity. These impressions were subsequently reproduced in stone and in religious paintings all over Asia. On the footprints are various auspicious Buddhist symbols. According to the *Vinaya Sutra*, the marks on the soles of the Buddha's foot were made by the tears of the sinful woman, Amrapati, and others who wept at Buddha's feet, to the indignation of his disciples.

Before the development of figural images of the Buddha in the first centuries AD, the Buddha's presence was indicated in stone carvings by several an-iconic (non-figural) symbols, including umbrellas (45), wheels (47), and the footprints of the Buddha. The Chinese pilgrim, Xuanzang (30) is known to have brought a drawing of the Buddha's footprints back to China with him from India in the seventh century. A stone marked with the Buddha's footprint, known as the Buddha's Foot Stone, is preserved at the Tiantai Monastery in the Western hills near Peiping in China.

Representations

The footprints of the Buddha are venerated in all Buddhist cultures, and in particular Sri Lanka and other countries that adopted the Southern tradition of Buddhism, since the Historical Buddha is the main focus of worship in this tradition. Although the Historical Buddha never visited these parts of Asia, he is believed to have visited certain sites in a prior existence, rendering these sites sacred. The footprints are usually carved or incised into stone, and are often protected within a special canopy.

The footprints usually bear distinguishing characteristics, either the wheel, or *chakra*, at the centre of the sole, or the 32, 108, or 132 distinctive signs of the Buddha. On many of the footprints are seven auspicious symbols (closely related to the Eight Auspicious Symbol [45]) known as the Seven Appearances: (1) a wheel, representing the teachings of the Buddha; (2) a crown, symbolizing the Buddha's supremacy over gods; (3) a conch shell, suggesting the preaching of the Law; (4) a vase, representing the Buddha's supreme intelligence; (5) fish, implying freedom from restraints; (6) a mace, symbolizing the divine force of the doctrine, and (7) flames, representing the Buddha's luminosity. Many footprints also bear the swastika motif (50).

One of the most famous representations of the Buddha's feet are the pair of feet carved into stone at Bodh Gaya (**ill. 1**). Copies of the Buddha's footprints were placed at important temples as objects of veneration. Rubbings were often made of these by worshippers who then took them home as sacred objects. In Japan, such footprints were also incorporated into the designs of souvenir prints given to worshippers who made donations to temples (**ill. 2, 3**). In some Southeast Asian images of the reclining Buddha, the soles of the Buddha's feet are incised with markings that resemble those on the footprints.

Buddhapada
  (Sanskrit)
bussoku
  (Japanese)

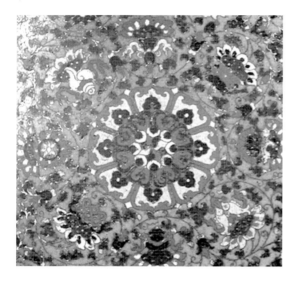

1 Pillar with Lion Capitol, India (above)

2 Wheel as one of the Eight Auspicious Symbols, cloisonné enamels, China, 15th or 16th century (above left)

3 Wheel of the Law as a detail of a Tibetan sand mandala, Tibet/USA, early 21st century (left)

Symbolism and Function

The wheel is one of the most important symbols in Buddhist art and iconography. It represents the endless cycle of birth, death and rebirth (70) known as samsara. It also symbolizes the dharma, or teaching, of the Buddha, which is in constant motion and provides a path towards spiritual enlightenment and eventual release from this cycle. Some Buddhists believe that the three main sections of the wheel – the hub, the spokes and the rim – represent the three kinds of training of Buddhist practice. The hub denotes the training in moral discipline, which supports and stabilizes the mind. The spokes symbolize the application of wisdom to in order to defeat ignorance. The rim represents the training in concentration, which holds the whole practice together.

The wheel appears in several forms that contain additional symbolic meaning. The wheel with four spokes represents the four great moments in the life of the Historical Buddha: his birth, departure from home, enlightenment and death. The wheel with eight spokes symbolizes the Noble Eightfold Path of Buddhism.

Representations

In early Buddhist art, the wheel often appeared alone as a symbol of the teachings of the Buddha, as in the case of the pillars built by the Indian Buddhist monarch Ashoka (c. 272–232 BC). On the tops of these pillars, four carved lions and four wheels faced the four directions to visually proclaim the Buddhist Law throughout India (**ill. 1**). Before human representations of the Buddha in Buddhist art in the late first centuries AD, the wheel often stood in the place of the Buddha to suggest his presence as well as his teachings. When human representations of the Buddha began to appear, the wheel was depicted on the palms of his hands and the soles of his feet, one of the Thirty-Two Marks of a Great Man (33), and it is also one of the Eight Auspicious Symbols (45) of Buddhism (**ill. 2**).

In the art of every Buddhist culture, the wheel appears as a motif in sculpture, paintings, architecture, and the decorative arts. It is a prominent motif in Tibetan art, where it is often flanked by two deer, the whole image representing the moment shortly after the Buddha's enlightenment when he delivered his first sermon to his disciples at the Deer Park at Sarnath. As such it appears as an element in Buddhist mandalas (73), geometric diagrams of perfected universes (**ill. 3**). In many sculptures and paintings of the Historical Buddha, Shakyamuni, is shown seated with his hands in the dharmachakra mudra (42), the 'turning of the Wheel of the Buddhist Law', a gesture which represents his first sermon. Although no wheel is actually depicted, it is formed by the position of his hands.

In some images of Buddhist deities, especially Tibetan wrathful deities, the deities brandish a wheel as a weapon to conquer evil and ignorance. This image of the wheel as a weapon may have been borrowed from earlier Hindu iconography where it is seen in the form of a disc as an attribute of the god Vishnu. In Hinduism, the disc was also taken to represent the absolute weapon that conquers desires and passions.

zhuanfalun
(Chinese)
temborin
(Japanese)
chonpobyun
(Korean)
dharmachakra
(Sanskrit)

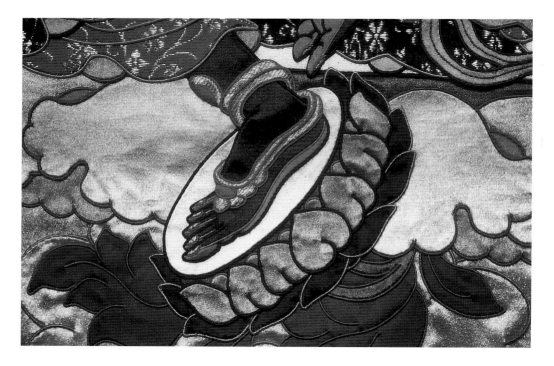

1 Lotus growing in Buddhist temple garden, Wakayama prefecture, Japan (top right)

2 Lotus at the centre of the Womb World Mandala, Japan (right)

3 Lotus on exterior of temple wall, Pulguksa, Korea (top left)

4 Foot of Green Tara on Lotus, Tibetan silk appliqué, 20th century (above)

Symbolism and Function

The lotus, one of the Eight Auspicious Symbols (45) of Buddhism, represents spiritual purity. Buddhists believe that just as the lotus flower rises up from the depths of muddy ponds and lakes to blossom immaculately above the water's surface, the human heart or mind can develop the virtues of the Buddha and transcend desires and attachments, to reveal its essentially pure nature. The unopened lotus, or lotus bud, is symbolic of the potential of all beings to attain Buddhahood or enlightenment. In esoteric Buddhism, the heart is often compared with an unopened lotus; when the virtues of the Buddha develop within the heart, the heart blossoms like a lotus (**ill. 1**).

In Tantric Buddhism, the lotus also represents the female sex organ, and therefore the feminine universal principle. In the Womb World Mandala (73), one of the two principal mandalas of esoteric Buddhism, the white lotus is found at the heart of the mandala, representing the womb of the world, from which everything emerged (**ill. 2**). This pure white lotus represents the state of total mental purity and spiritual perfection, or bodhi. It has eight petals, symbolizing the Eightfold Path of Buddhism.

Lotuses of other colours represent various associations. The pink lotus, the supreme lotus, is the lotus of the Historical Buddha, Shakyamuni (1). The red lotus, shown fully open, represents the original nature of the heart and symbolizes love, compassion and passion. It is the lotus of Avalokiteshvara (8). The blue lotus, shown partially open, symbolizes wisdom, knowledge and the victory of the spirit over the senses. It is the lotus of Manjushri (12) and of Prajnaparamita (24), the embodiment of the perfection of wisdom.

Representations

Lotuses appear in every aspect of Buddhist art in all Buddhist cultures, from the real lotuses in temple gardens to the lotus thrones (36) that support the Buddhas, bodhisattvas, and deities. Lotuses are an important element of Buddhist decoration in general, and scrolling lotuses embellish Buddhist textiles, ceramics and architecture (**ill. 3**). Buddhas and bodhisattvas are often depicted in painting and sculpture seated on a lotus in full bloom, symbolizing the divine birth and the perfected spiritual state of the being. The lotus may be shown attached to a stem that rises up from a pond below, particularly in depictions of Amitabha (6). In some images of standing Buddhas or bodhisattvas, each foot rests on a separate lotus (**ill. 4**).

In paintings of Buddhist paradises, in particular the Western Paradise (72) of Amitabha, there is a pond with lotuses in the foreground. The souls of devotees to Amitabha are believed to be reborn on these lotuses, the more virtuous of which are reborn into open lotuses and can immediately receive Amitabha's help in attaining enlightenment. Less virtuous souls are reborn into closed lotuses, and must wait until the flower blooms before receiving Amitabha's aid.

padma
   (Sanskrit)
lianhua
   (Chinese)
renge
   (Japanese)
padma
   (Tibetan)
kiem lien,
   hoa sen
   (Vietnamese)

1 Precious jewel, Tibet (above)

2 Three Precious Jewels, appliqué, Tibet, 20th century (below)

3 Kshitigharbha holding a precious jewel, wood with polychrome with inlaid rock crystal eyes, Japan, 13th century (right)

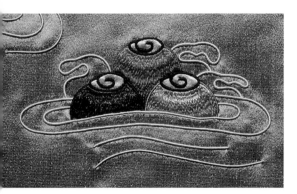

Symbolism and Function

The precious jewel in Buddhism is said to be able to grant all wishes or satisfy all desires, and so is also known as the 'Wish-granting Jewel'. According to Buddhist legend, the jewel is one of Seven Jewels of Royal Power, the Saptaratna, of the Universal King, or Chakravartin. (The other six are the precious wheel, the precious elephant, the precious horse, the precious queen, the precious minister, the precious general.) The jewel was believed to give the Universal King the power to see and obtain everything, just as the Buddha has the power to see and understand all things.

Although originally a symbol of material wealth, in the context of Buddhism, the precious jewel usually represents spiritual wealth. The shining jewel, with its power to clarify the heart, represents all the treasures of Buddhism, in particular the understanding of the Buddhist Law. It can also represent the concept of spiritual enlightenment itself, the most desirable and sought after of all things.

Representations

The jewel is usually represented in the form of a round ball with a pointed top and horizontal bands near the top (**ill. 1**). It is sometimes shown alone, but can also be grouped in threes, representing the three jewels, or triratna, of Buddhism: the Buddha, the dharma, or Law, and the sangha, or monastic community (**ill. 2**). The single jewel or group of three jewels may be placed on a lotus throne or on a cloud or be surrounded by flames. The triple jewels are sometimes placed at the top of an instrument such as a magic staff that is used in esoteric rituals.

The jewel is often an attribute of a particular Buddha, bodhisattva or deity. For example, the bodhisattva Kshitigarbha (11) is almost always shown holding a monk's staff in his right hand and a single jewel in his left hand (**ill. 3**). An esoteric form of Avalokiteshvara (8), known as Chintamanichakra Avalokiteshvara, or 'Avalokiteshvara of the Wheel of the Wish-granting Jewel', was popular in China and Japan as a figure of private devotion. The figure usually appeared in a relaxed pose, holding a wheel, and a wish-granting jewel close to his breast. In some images, the jewels are in front of him on a small lotus throne, while in other examples, they are placed in his crown.

Other deities hold jewels for different reasons. For example, the deity Vaishravana or Kubera (19) is often shown with a mongoose spewing out jewels, symbolizing the deity's status as God of Wealth. Although on the surface, this deity and his jewels appear to grant material abundance to his worshippers, on a deeper level they symbolize the spiritual wealth that can be obtained by following the Buddha's teachings.

chintamani,
  mani, ratna
  (Sanskrit)
ruyizhu *(Chinese)*
hoshu, nyo-i-shu
  (Japanese)
nor-bu rin-po-
  che *(Tibetan)*

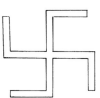

1 Swastika, Tibet (above)

2 Seated Buddha with sauvastika on chest (detail), gilded bronze, Korea, 16th century (left)

3 Swastika motif on a carpet, wool and cotton, Tibet, 19th century (below left)

4 Sauvastika pattern on textile, Bali, Indonesia, 20th century (below)

Symbolism and Function

The swastika or svastika consists of a cross with the four ends bent at right angles and directed to the right, so as to rotate clockwise (**ill. 1**). It is a symbol of good fortune in the artistic vocabulary of many cultures, and has been found in the art of the Egyptians, Romans, and Celts, as well as that of Native Americans, the Persians, and the ancient Greeks. In India, the symbol is seen on artifacts from the Indus Valley Civilization, as early as 2500 BC, and is generally considered to be a symbol of the sun, probably derived from the clockwise motion of the sun. The name svastika, or swastika, is derived from the Sanskrit root sv-asti, meaning well-being, good fortune, success or prosperity. In Hindu belief, the swastika became identified with the god Vishnu, as a symbol of his solar disc and was a mark that often appeared on Vishnu's chest. The sign was also associated with one of the other major Hindu gods, Shiva, and the snake cults of the Naga, possibly because of similar markings on the cobra's hood.

In Buddhist symbolism, the swastika is considered to be the symbol or seal of the Buddha's heart and is believed to contain within it the whole mind of the Buddha. This sign is said to be the first of the sixty-five auspicious signs on the footprint of the Buddha, while the sauvastika, which turns in a counter-clockwise direction, is the fourth sign. In the indigenous Bon tradition of Tibet, the swastika is an important symbol of the eternal or unchanging. However, the Bon swastika rotates in a counter-clockwise direction. It was the counter-clockwise sauvastika that the Nazis of twentieth-century Germany adopted as their symbol.

In China, the symbol was probably the ancient form of the character, fang, meaning the four directions of the world. Later, from about 700 AD, it came to represent the number ten thousand, meaning infinity, and most often stands for ten thousand years of good fortune, particularly within the context of Daoism. It is frequently used instead of wan, the Chinese character for this number.

Representations

In Buddhist art, the swastika or the sauvastika appear on a range of objects and in a variety of materials. In sculptural art, it may appear on the breast of images of the Buddha, representing the seal of the heart of the Buddha (**ill. 2**). It also appear on the palms or the soles of the feet. The motif is most commonly seen in the decorative arts of China and cultures under its influence, where it represents good fortune (**ill. 3**). In Buddhist and secular textile decoration, a pattern formed by numerous linked swastikas or sauvastikas often forms the background or border design for a central design (**ill. 4**). For example, this design can often be seen on the decorative silk mounts or borders around Buddhist paintings, and altar cloths and other such textiles used in Buddhist temples, often feature such a design. The motif can also be found in metalwork and on porcelain.

wanzi *(Chinese)*
manji *(Japanese)*
gyung-drung,
   geg-gsang
   (Tibetan)

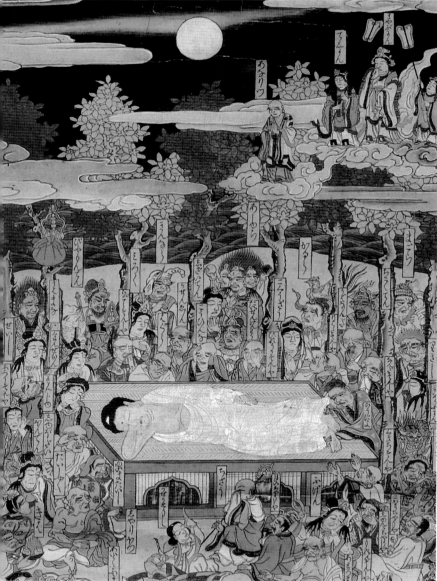

1 Queen Maya giving birth under a teak tree, Gandhara (above)

2 The bodhi tree, Bodh Gaya, India (below)

3 Shakyamuni dying in a grove of sala trees, woodblock print (detail), Japan (left)

Symbolism and Function

Trees played an extremely important role in the life of the Historical Buddha, Shakyamuni (1), and are present at his birth, enlightenment and his death. In particular, the tree under which the Buddha attained enlightenment, a pipal tree in Bodh Gaya, India (74), is still revered today as the site of the Buddha's spiritual awakening and as a symbol of enlightenment itself.

According to Buddhist legend, the mother of Prince Siddhartha, Queen Maya gave birth to the Buddha in a miraculous manner in a grove of trees in Lumbini. When she knew she was about to give birth, she grasped the branch of a teak tree with her right hand, and from her right side the baby emerged. Later, after years of searching for spiritual release under various teachers, Siddhartha arrived at a place now known as Bodh Gaya, where a pipal tree (ficus religiosa) had sprouted on the day of Siddhartha's birth. Recognizing the tree, Siddhartha sat down beneath it prepared to meditate until he achieved spiritual release. Siddhartha remained under the tree for several weeks in a state of deep concentration until he achieved nirvana, or enlightenment. The final moments of the Buddha's life are also represented among trees. When the Buddha was eighty or eighty-one years old, he suffered from food poisoning and retreated to a grove of sala trees (shorea robusta) in Kushinagara in modern Bihar. There, under the sala trees and surrounded by his faithful disciples, he passed away and entered a state of final enlightenment or parinirvana.

Representations

The tree under which the Buddha is born can be seen in the art of most Buddhist cultures in painted and sculpted scenes of the life of the Buddha. In general, Queen Maya is depicted grasping the tree with her right hand, as the infant Buddha emerges from her side (**ill. 1**). The most commonly represented tree in Buddhist imagery is the bodhi tree under which Prince Siddhartha attained enlightenment. A descendant from the original bodhi tree is at Bodh Gaya in India and is still revered by Buddhists from all around the world (**ill. 2**). A similar tree, believed to descend from a cutting of the original tree brought to Anuradhapura in Sri Lanka by the son of King Ashoka, is also an object of reverence. This scene is captured in the sculpture and painting in all Buddhist cultures. Siddhartha is shown seated in the lotus position (38) under a very low and wide tree full with leaves. Finally, in scenes of the Buddha's death, he is depicted lying in a grove of tall, thin sala trees, with gold or yellow leaves (**ill. 3**).

Trees appear in other aspects of Buddhist art, including scenes of the Buddhist Paradises (72), in which trees are shown laden with jewels, representing the spiritual wealth of those who are progressing towards enlightenment. There is also a tree, the Rose-Apple Tree, on the summit of Mount Meru at the very centre of the Buddhist cosmos, serving as a cosmic pillar connecting heaven and earth. At the centre of Buddhist reliquaries, or stupas, there is traditionally a tall wooden pole that is set deep into the ground and rises up out of the top of the stupa. Like the tree, this pole also denotes the axis mundi, or cosmic pillar.

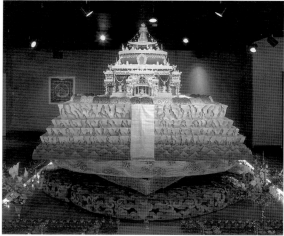

1 Shakyamuni preaching on Vulture Peak, silver/gilt/bronze, Kashmir, 5th or 6th century (left)

2 Mount Meru at the centre of the Buddhist Universe, Tibet (above)

3 The Shi-tro Mandala on Mount Meru, Tibet (top)

Symbolism and Function

In most religions, mountains play an important symbolic role, since they are the geographical points at which followers believe they can be closest to their gods or to the highest powers in the universe. Several mountains feature in the life of the Buddha and in the mythology and cosmology of Buddhism. This is no doubt in part because the Buddhist faith was born in the foothills of the Himalayas, and several important events in the Historical Buddha's life took place near or on mountains. For example, the Buddha sat at the top of the Vulture Peak in northern India to deliver many important sermons, the most famous of which were the teachings that became the *Lotus Sutra*.

Certain mythical mountains feature prominently in the cosmology of Buddhism. In particular, the sacred Mount Meru is believed to be at the very centre of the universe, and serves as the axis of the universe, a cosmic pillar that connects earth with the heavens. This mountain is a mythical peak that that has its origins in Hindu cosmology and was also inherited by the Jains. Many Buddhist deities are believed to reside in mountain paradises. For example, Manjushri (12), the bodhisattva of wisdom, is believed to live on a five-peaked mountain, either in the Himalayas or in China. The Tibetan spiritual leader Padmasambhava (29) is believed to live in the Copper Mountain Paradise.

Representations

The Buddha's sermon on the Vulture Peak that became the *Lotus Sutra* was particularly important to those Mahayana Buddhists, including the Chinese Tiantai sect and the Japanese Tendai and Nichiren sects, who perceived this to be his most important teaching. This scene is represented in images of Shakyamuni (1) seated in monk's robes at the summit of the mountain flanked by two bodhisattvas and preaching to the sage-like arhats (27) below. In some sculptures, Vulture Peak is not depicted but merely implied by the presence of vultures on the Buddha's throne (**ill. 1**).

Mount Meru is often depicted in cosmic diagrams created to explain the structure of the Buddhist universe. Meru is usually shown as a vertical peak rising up out of a ring of seven mountains (**ill. 2**). On its upper slopes are cities of demigods and the Four Heavenly Kings (18), and at the very top is Sudarshana, the realm of the most important Hindu gods and the Indian equivalent of the Greek Mount Olympus. Around Mount Meru are the other continents of the universe extending in the four directions.

The sacred mountain is often a component of the mandalas of the esoteric schools of Buddhism. The perfected environments of the central Buddhas, bodhisattvas, and other deities of the mandalas are often situated on top of Mount Meru or other mountains. Although these mountains are not always clearly discernible in two-dimensional representations of mandalas, they are clearly visible in three-dimensional mandalas, which closely resemble celestial palaces on top of great sacred mountains (**ill. 3**).

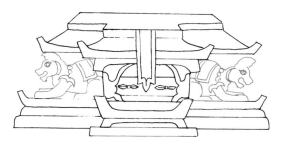

1 Lion throne of the Buddha (left)

2 Lions guarding the entrance to the Mahamuni Pagoda, Mandalay, Burma, 19th century (above)

3 Pair of deer, gilded copper, Tibet, 18th century (below left)

4 Queen Maya's Dream of a White Elephant, India (below)

Lions

In Indian iconography, the lion has long been a symbol of royalty and power, so the presence of a lion on images of the Buddha partly suggests the royal origins of the Historical Buddha (1). In fact, after his enlightenment, the Buddha was often referred to as the 'Lion of the Shakyas', or Shakyasimha, an acknowledgment of his immense spiritual power. The lion, therefore, often represents the power of the Buddha's teachings, or dharma, and lions have often been portrayed roaring out the dharma for all to hear, as on the pillars built at Sarnath and other locations by King Ashoka (third century BC) to proclaim the Buddha's Law. Thrones supporting the Historical Buddha are often decorated with lions (**ill. 1**).

The lion serves as a mount for certain deities. Manjushri (12), the bodhisattva of wisdom, rides a lion, symbolizing the power of the Buddhist Law. At the entrance to some temples, particularly in East and Southeast Asia, stand a pair of lion-like creatures, often known by their Chinese name, fo, or 'Buddha' lions, or dogs (**ill. 2**). Like the Gate Guardians (20), these lions protect the Buddhist Law and the temples. In the Himalayas, the lion is replaced by the snow lion, which is native to that region.

simha (Sanskrit)
shishi (Japanese)
nghe (Vietnamese)
singh (Thai)

Deer

In Buddhist art, deer symbolize the Deer Park at Sarnath in northern India, where the Historical Buddha gave his first sermon after attaining enlightenment. This park is, therefore, associated with the original dissemination of the Buddha's teachings, which later evolved into the religion of Buddhism. The Buddha is often depicted seated on a throne decorated with two deer sitting facing each other, and in Tibet, in particular, two deer are often shown flanking the Wheel of the Law (42) (**ill. 3**).

shika (Japanese)
khwang (Thai)

Elephants

Although the elephant has an important role in legends about the birth of the Buddha, this creature plays a relatively minor role in Buddhist iconography. According to legend, the Buddha's mother, Queen Maya had a dream that she was being impregnated by a white elephant, a scene in the life of the Buddha which has been portrayed quite frequently (ill. 4). Soon afterwards, she became pregnant, and gave birth to the Buddha. The white elephant was a sign that she was to give birth to an extraordinary child and future Buddha. In Buddhist iconography, the bodhisattva, Samantabhadra (13) also rides a white elephant.

hastin (Sanskrit)
zo (Japanese)
glang-po
  (Tibetan)
voi (Vietnamese)
chang (Thai)

Horses

According to Buddhist legend, the Prince Siddhartha escaped from his father's palace riding a horse. His attendants, or the Hindu gods, or the Four Heavenly Kings (18), each picked up one leg of the horse so that its hooves would not make a sound. This scene is often portrayed in images of the life of the Historical Buddha, Shakyamuni.

ashva (Sanskrit)
ma (Chinese)
uma (Japanese)
tra-mchog
  (Tibetan)

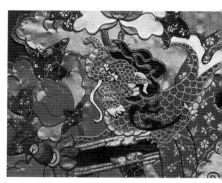

1 The Buddha sheltered by Muchalinda, stone, Khmer, 12th century (left)

2 Dragon water fountain, Buddhist temple, Wakayama, Japan (below left)

3 Makara, Tibetan silk appliqué thangka, 20th century (below right)

4 Garuda holding a Snake, Tibetan silk appliqué, 20th century (bottom)

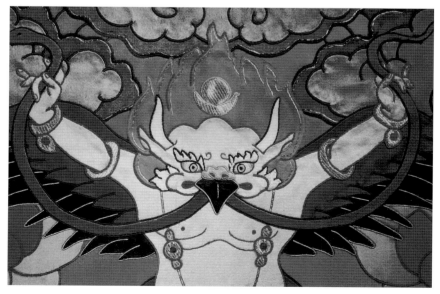

Snakes, Serpents and Dragons

In India, the snake or serpent is an ancient symbol of water and the underworld, and snake deities, or nagas, have long been considered guardians of the treasures of the earth and attributed with supernatural powers, including the control of rainfall and protection against fires. In Buddhism, snake deities are benevolent minor deities and feature in several Buddhist legends. In one, a naga king called Muchalinda offered protection to the meditating Buddha during a storm just before his enlightenment. The naga, most likely a cobra, coiled himself around the Buddha and transformed his hood into a protective umbrella over the Buddha's head (**ill. 1**). In another legend, a naga king disguised himself as a human being in order to hear the Buddha's teachings. In Buddhist painting and sculpture, snakes are often the attributes of certain deities, particularly wrathful deities who often wear them around their necks. Snakes also appear as symbolic decorative elements on Buddhist ritual objects.

In China, Japan, and Southeast Asia, the dragon is a benign creature that inhabits the seas, rivers, lakes and clouds and has very similar qualities to the Indian naga. Dragons appear in the Buddhist art of these regions, often as decorative elements in temples, for example as roof ornaments, protecting the buildings from fire, or as water fountains at the entrance to temples (**ill. 2**).

Sea Monsters

In many Buddhist sculptures and paintings, the head of a sea monster, known most commonly as a makara, is a prominent decorative detail in painting, sculpture and architecture (**ill. 3**). This sea monster, with a composite elephant-crocodile head and the body of a fish, appears in the iconography of the Himalayan region and Southeast Asia in particular, most often as a head from whose mouth issues another decorative element. In Tibetan metalwork, for example, one of the elements of certain forms of the vajra (55) is the makara head from which the prongs of the vajra emerge. In much Southeast Asian temple architecture, makaras appear above doorways, often on either side of a demonic face known as a kirtimukkha, or 'Face of Glory'. These motifs serve a protective function, preventing evil from entering the building.

Mythical Birds

In India, the Himalayas, and Southeast Asia, Garuda, the bird-like vehicle of the Hindu god Vishnu, appears as a decorative detail in architecture and sculpture. In Buddhist mythology, the garudas are the immortal enemies of the nagas, and are often shown grasping a snake in their hands or beaks (**ill. 4**). In East Asia, the phoenix, which probably originated in early Chinese mythology, is represented in Buddhist art, for example at the Byodoin temple near Kyoto in Japan, where many of the temple's decorative elements are in the form of this bird, representing the concept of rebirth in the Western Pure Land (72) of Amitabha (6), the principal figure worshipped at this temple.

naga *(Sanskrit)*
long *(Chinese)*
ryu *(Japanese)*
neak *(Khmer)*
lus
   (Mongolian)
phi *(Thai)*
klu *(Tibetan)*

makatsu-gu
   (Japanese)
makara
   (Sanskrit)
ma-ka-ra
   (Tibetan)

1 Vajra bell, or vajraghanta, bronze, Tibet, 19th century (far left)

2 Three-pointed vajra, Tibet (above left)

3 Crossed vajras, Tibet (below left)

4 Crossed vajras forming the base of the Shi-tro Mandala, sand, USA/Tibet, 2001 (below)

Symbolism and Function

The vajra, often translated as either 'diamond' or 'thunderbolt', is one of the most important of all Buddhist symbols, and is the main symbol of Vajrayana, or 'Vajra Vehicle', Buddhism. This short metal weapon has the nature of a diamond, as it can cut through any substance but cannot itself be cut, and it has the irresistible force of a thunderbolt. As such, it has come to represent firmness of spirit as well as spiritual power. This weapon has an ancient history in India and further afield, even appearing on effigies in Mesopotamia. In India, the vajra was first used in Vedic (pre-Hindu) rituals and was the favourite weapon of the powerful Hindu god, Indra. In Buddhism, the weapon can be interpreted symbolically as one which can destroy the enemies of the Buddhist Law. It can also symbolize, particularly in esoteric Buddhist sects, the power of knowledge over ignorance and of the spirit over the passions.

In many Tantric Buddhist practices, especially in the Himalayan region, the vajra symbolizes the male sexual organ, the male cosmic force and the quality of compassion. The bell (58) symbolizes the female organ, the female cosmic principle and the virtue of wisdom. Some Buddhist deities hold a vajra in one hand, and a bell in the other, symbolizing the union of these two forces and of wisdom and compassion. The vajra and bell may also be united in one object, the vajra bell, or vajraghanta, with the vajra functioning as the handle of the bell (**ill. 1**). This combination also represents the two great mandalas (73) of esoteric Buddhism, the Diamond World (Sanskrit: Vajradhatu) Mandala, and the Womb World (Sanskrit: Garbhadhatu) Mandala. The vajra can also be paired with the lotus, with the vajra again representing the male force and knowledge, while the lotus (48) represents the female force and innate reason.

Representations

The vajra is an important instrument in esoteric Buddhist rituals. Usually cast in bronze and often gilded, it comes in several variations, the most common being the three-pointed vajra (**ill. 2**). Many vajras are decorated with symbolic details such as lotus petals around the bell-shaped section, or precious jewels (49) at either end. In the three-pointed vajras, the three points are often depicted emerging from the mouths of sea monsters called makaras (54). There are also vajras with one, two, four, five, or nine points, each having distinct symbolism and functions.

The vajra often appears as the principal attribute of an esoteric Buddhist deity such as Vajrapani (14), who wields the vajra to defeat the enemies of Buddhism. It also appears in multiple form as one of the protective rings around the central section of certain mandalas. The circle of vajras, which lies inside the circle of flames, must be passed through mentally during meditation in order to enter into the central section of the mandala. Sometimes two vajras are crossed to form a sort of wheel (47) (**ill. 3**). These double vajras create four points that represent the four directions of the cosmos. This form is often used at the centre of Buddhist mandalas, with the tips of the vajras showing at the mandala's four directional gates (**ill. 4**).

vajra (Sanskrit)
jingangchu
  (Chinese)
kongo-sho
  (Japanese)
rdo-rje, dorje
  (Tibetan)

1 Acalanatha with sword, embroidered silk, Japan, 20th century (above)

2 Vaishravana holding a lance in his right hand, woodblock print, Japan, 18th century (left)

3 Axe, Japan (right)

4 Ritual Axe, gilt copper alloy and rock crystal, Tibet, 17th century or earlier (below)

Symbolism and Function

ayudha *(Sanskrit)*
wuqi *(Chinese)*
buki *(Japanese)*

Many Buddhas, bodhisattvas and other deities of the Mahayana and Vajrayana sects are depicted carrying weapons of various types and magical instruments, symbolizing their various powers against the enemies of Buddhism. They also represent the protection that is offered to devotees by the Buddha and his Law.

Swords

Many deities brandish swords as symbols of their ability to cut through ignorance and evil. They often hold them up in the air as if slashing at some unseen force. The bodhisattvas Akashagharba (10) and Manjushri (12) are both often shown holding a sword to represent their wisdom and the supreme knowledge of the Buddha. Acalanatha, one of the Kings of Mystical Knowledge (21), is always shown standing among flames and holding a sword in his right hand (**ill. 1**). Many of the swords held by deities have a hilt in the form of a vajra (55), the vajra also representing the indestructible power of the Buddhist Law. The blade of the sword replaces the central point of the vajra.

Spears, Lances, Tridents and Axes

Spears are attributes of certain male deities and are generally associated with fire and virility. They also represent the triumph of the power of good and truth over ignorance. The Guardian of the North, Vaishravana (19), is generally depicted wielding a spear or lance in his right hand (**ill. 2**). Tridents are also important weapons and symbolize the Three Jewels (49) of Buddhism (the Buddha, the dharma, and the sangha). Avalokiteshvara (8) is often shown holding a three-pointed staff resembling a trident. The axe is wielded by wrathful deities as a weapon that destroys obstacles blocking the path towards wisdom and enlightenment (**ill. 3**). It is also used symbolically by priests in Tibetan Buddhist rituals (**ill. 4**).

Bows and Arrows

Certain deities are depicted holding a bow and arrow, a symbol of intense concentration and the destruction of the passions. The bow and arrow can also represent the passions themselves, especially carnal love, and it is the attribute of one of the Kings of Mystical Knowledge, Ragavidyaraja, 'Conqueror of the Passions'.

Staffs

Some bodhisattvas and guardian figures carry staffs of the type carried traditionally by monks and beggars. Sometimes known as staffs of wisdom, these staffs appear in the Buddhist art of Tibet and East Asia. They generally have a metal ring-like section at the top, from which dangle several more rings. Traditionally, these staffs were used by itinerant monks and beggars to scare off snakes and other wild animals and to warn people of the approach of a holy man. The bodhisattva, Kshitigarbha (11), who is generally depicted in monk's garb, usually carries such a staff.

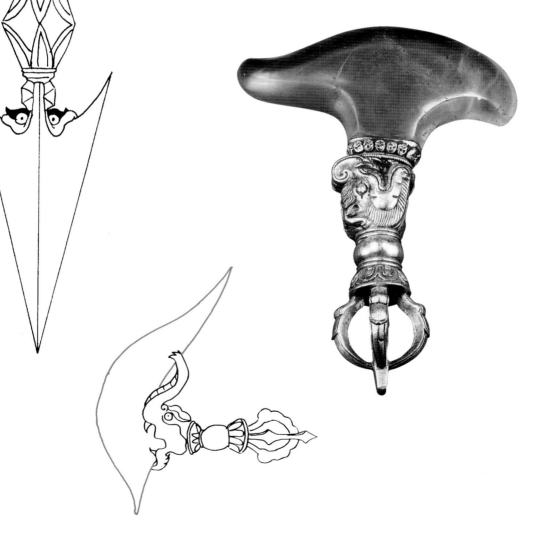

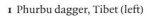

1 Phurbu dagger, Tibet (left)

2 Chopper, Tibet (below)

3 Ritual chopper, gilt copper alloy and rock crystal, Eastern Tibet, Derge (?), 17th century or earlier (below right)

Daggers

Symbolism and Function

kila *(Sanskrit)*
phur-bu,
   phur-pa
   (Tibetan)

The magic dagger is one of the most important and most mysterious of the Tibetan Buddhist ritual objects. It is most commonly used by priests and shamans in Tibetan Buddhist rituals to expel demonic forces and disease. This dagger is a short weapon or nail with a triangular blade and a hilt in the form of a vajra surmounted by a head. The origin of this ritual weapon is unknown, but it is believed by some Tibetan Buddhists to have been invented by the guru Padmasambhava (29) in the eighth century. He is said to have stabbed a nail or dagger into the ground to pin down the evil spirits and thus consecrate the ground on which he established Tibet's Samye monastery. It is most likely that this weapon with its three sides is derived from the nails or pegs that were used in the Himalayan region to hold the rope stays of a tent in place.

Representations

Most ritual daggers are made of metal, wood, or ivory, and many are decorated with inlaid precious stones. At the centre of the hilt of many daggers is a vajra, at either end of which are makaras (54), or mythical sea creatures, from whose mouths emerge the three blades of the dagger. Along each surface of the blade is often the image of a snake, which descends towards the tip of the blade. The dagger may be crowned with one or three wrathful faces of the deity of the dagger (**ill. 1**).

Choppers

Symbolism and Function

karttrika
   (Sanskrit)
gri-gug
   (Tibetan)

The chopper, or cleaver, is a ritual weapon with a crescent-shaped blade and a handle at the centre of the curve (**ill. 2**). This weapon primarily belongs to the esoteric imagery and rituals of Tibet, where it is used symbolically to cut away ignorance. It is also employed in rituals of exorcism by priests and shamans.

Representations

Choppers are usually made of metal and often have elaborately ornamented handles, with designs also appearing on the inside curve of the blade. In some examples, the blade is carved out of a second material such as rock crystal (**ill. 3**). Male and female wrathful Buddhist deities are shown in paintings and sculptures wielding choppers which they use to threaten or chop up enemies of the Law. For example, Vajravarahi, the female consort of Samvara (22) is typically represented wielding a chopper in her right hand and a staff of wisdom (56) in her left. The chopper is often paired with the skull cup (60), as the chopper symbolizes cutting through ignorance, while the blood in the skull cup symbolizes wisdom. The deity Yamantaka (16), the wrathful manifestation of Manjushri (12), the bodhisattva of wisdom, is often depicted holding a chopper in his right hand and a skull cup full of blood in his left.

1 *Vajraghanta*, combination of vajra and bell, Tibet (below)

2 Drum, wood and skin, Tibet, 19th century (above right)

3 Trumpet, copper, brass and turquoise, Tibet, 18th century (above left)

4 Conch Shell, silver, coral, jade, turquoise and cotton tassels, Tibet, 18th century (left)

Musical instruments do not generally appear as the attributes or symbols of the Buddhas, bodhisattvas or major Buddhist deities. Occasionally, however, an esoteric deity such as Sarasvati (24), is shown holding an instrument that signifies her role as a goddess of music and learning. Most Buddhist musical instruments were adopted by the esoteric schools of Tibet, Nepal, and Japan, and are used in rituals.

Bells

Bells are used in esoteric Buddhist rituals to symbolize sound or the vibrations generated by the repetition of mantras. Bells and vajras (55) often appear together, representing the female and male aspects of the universe respectively. In Tibetan Buddhist rituals, the priest or lama holds a vajra in his right hand and a bell in his left and unifies them by crossing his arms over his chest to represent the enlightened mind. Esoteric deities of the Vajrayana tradition of the Himalayas and Japan are often shown holding a bell in one hand and a vajra in the other. In some cases, the bell and vajra are united in a single object, the vajraghanta, in which the handle of the bell is a vajra (**ill. 1**). This form represents the union of wisdom (female) and compassion (male).

Drums

Various cymbals, gongs and drums are used in esoteric Buddhist rituals. In Tibet, the use of the drum in Buddhist rituals probably originates in the ecstatic music of older shamanistic rituals, which helped to transport shamans to the realm of the spirits, and also warded off evil spirits. The most common are drums made of wood or even human skulls, the peaks of which are joined together and the open ends covered with animal skins (**ill. 2**). Some small double-sided drums have a weight attached to a cord, and by flicking the wrist the user can alternately strike both sides of the drum. Certain Buddhist deities are shown holding this type of drum.

Trumpets, Horns and Conch Shells

Trumpets, horns and other wind instruments have long been blown to dispel evil and to represent the sound of the Buddhist Law. Particularly in Tibet, the trumpet is a very important part of the music that accompanies sacred ceremonies. Trumpets and horns are often made out of bronze or another metal, but in some cases, they are made from human or animal bone, in particular the thigh bone. The far end of the trumpet is often ornately decorated with Buddhist motifs created in silver, gilded bronze and inlaid jewels. In some examples, the face of a makara (54), or mythical water creature is used to decorate the bone trumpet (**ill. 3**).

One of the Eight Auspicious Symbols (45) of Buddhism, the conch shell has long been used in India and the Himalayas to call together a congregation. Its sound represents the spreading of the Law by the voice of the Buddha. In Tibet and Nepal, many conch shells are decorated with metalwork and inlaid precious jewels (**ill. 4**).

1 Water ewer, silver, crystal, turquoise, and opal, Central Tibet, 18th century (right)

2 Four patriarchs of Shingon Buddhism, hand coloured woodblock print, Japan, 17th century (left)

3 Flower vases in a mandala, Yamantaka Mandala (detail), colours in silk, Tibet, *c.* 1700 (below)

Water Containers

Symbolism and Function

Water is a key element in Buddhist rituals of all traditions and cultures and is present on all temple altars. During various Buddhist rituals, the officiating monk or priest uses a vessel with a handle and spout to sprinkle water on the image of the deity and all people attending the ritual, including himself. The water has a symbolic cleansing function, washing away all impurities that block the way to enlightenment.

Representations

Such sprinkling vessels are usually made out of metal in the Himalayan region or ceramic in East and Southeast Asia. They are generally tall and elegant with a long, narrow neck, a curved handle and spout, and a small lid. The metalwork examples are often ornamented with inlaid shell or precious stones, while the ceramic examples generally have painted, incised or inlaid decoration, most commonly of lotuses or other Buddhist symbols (**ill. 1**). Sprinkling vessels also appear as attributes of particular Buddhist deities. The bodhisattva of compassion, Avalokiteshvara (8), is often depicted seated in a natural setting with a sprinkling vessel, or similar water container, on a rock nearby. This vessel is believed to contain the nectar of his compassion, which is given to quench the thirst of his believers. In some depictions of Buddhist monks or patriarchs, a similar water vessel is shown at their side (**ill. 2**).

The conch shell (58) is commonly used in Tibetan Buddhist rituals as a container for consecrated water. Conch shells are often placed on top of water pots on the altar. Many Tibetan conch shells are decorated with elaborate metalwork details, often featuring inlaid precious materials, including coral and turquoise.

Flower Vases

Symbolism and Function

Flower vases are often present on Buddhist altars. Flowers are important offerings to the deity being worshipped, and the vase is also considered an important part of the offering. The choice of flower is often symbolic, such as the lotus (48), which denotes purity and enlightenment. The vases are also full of symbolism, often representing the concept of a treasure vase, one of the Eight Auspicious Symbols (45) of Buddhism.

Representations

Traditionally Buddhist flower vases are round with narrow necks and a wide mouth. They are most often made of bronze or ceramic and may feature incised or painted designs, often of lotuses. Flower vases are often placed at the four corners and the centre of a shrine, symbolizing the Five Dhyani Buddhas, or transcendental Buddhas. They also appear as symbolic motifs in mandalas (73), where they are placed at either side of the directional gates (**ill. 3**).

1 Siddhartha throwing golden
rice bowl into the river, Burma
(above)

2 Skull cup, silver gilt, Tibet,
18th century (below)

Begging Bowl

Symbolism and Function

The begging bowl, or alms bowl, is probably the simplest but most important object in the daily lives of the monks of many Buddhist sects, particularly those of the Southern traditions. Many monks depend on lay support for their daily sustenance and carry a bowl around with them in which to collect alms, either in the form of money or food.

Although the bowl is primarily a practical object in the Buddhist world, it also possesses symbolic qualities associated with the life of the Historical Buddha, Shakyamuni (1). According to one Buddhist legend, when Siddhartha began his meditation under the bodhi tree, a young woman named Sujata, believing that he was the divinity of the tree, offered him a golden bowl full of succulent boiled rice. Knowing that his enlightenment was imminent, Shakyamuni divided the rice into 49 portions, one for each day leading up to his enlightenment, and because a monk is not allowed any belongings, he then threw the bowl into the river (**ill. 1**). Because of this and other legends, the simple food bowl is often regarded as a symbol of the Buddha and his teachings.

Representations

In general, Buddhist alms bowls are very plain vessels, but elaborate examples crafted out of ceramic, metal, lacquer and other materials also exist. Bowls are depicted in the visual representations of certain figures. For example, in certain images of Shakyamuni, he is sitting holding a monk's begging bowl in his left hand and touching the earth (43) with his right. Amitabha (6) and Bhaishajyaguru (2) are also occasionally shown holding bowls.

Skull Cup

Symbolism and Function

Skull cups, often made using human skulls, are used primarily in Tibetan Buddhist rituals and are often seen in the hands of wrathful Buddhist deities in Tibetan sculptures and paintings. They are used in Tibetan tantric Buddhist rituals as symbols of the wrathful deities. In these rituals, lamas and other eminent practitioners drink consecrated alcoholic beverages or sometimes even blood from such cups, probably symbolizing the wrathful deity drinking the blood of his or her victim.

Representations

Skull cups are often formed from a human cranium which has been cut into shape, lined with a metal rim and ornamented. Many skull cups, however, are simply made out of a precious metal in the form of a cranium. They often feature elaborate decoration, including Buddhist symbols such as lotuses and vajras (48, 55), and many have lids that are also heavily ornamented. Some have feet in the form of human skulls.

patra
(Sanskrit)
bo *(Chinese)*
hachi
(Japanese)

kapala
(Sanskrit)

1 Buddhist altar with offerings and incense, Wat Arun, Bangkok, Thailand (left)

2 Celadon glazed incense burner, 13th century, China (below)

3 Incense burner with lion finial, Korea, 13th century (above left)

4 Figure carrying incense burner with handles, Japan (left)

Symbolism and Function

Probably the most universal of Buddhist ritual vessels, incense burners, or censers, are used in all Buddhist cultures. The burning of incense as an offering to the Buddha or during a Buddhist ritual is performed both in the home and in the temple. The lighting of incense is an important act of ritual fumigation that is believed by many practitioners to clear the air of evil spirits. In addition, followers of certain Buddhist traditions, particularly the esoteric traditions of Tibet and Japan, have made offerings to Buddhist deities associated with all five senses. Incense and flowers provide a pleasant olfactory offering to the deities.

In most cases, incense sticks containing sweet-smelling herbs and spices are lit by the priest or the worshipper and placed upright in sand inside a large, round open container. These incense burners are usually placed on the altar with flowers and other offerings in front of the Buddhist figure being venerated (**ill. 1**).

Representations

Incense burners take various different forms and are created out of a wide range of materials depending on the region. Most incense burners are open vessels, much like a deep bowl, with a handle on each side. They are most often made out of a metal such as bronze or copper and decorated with gilding or sometimes enamel details. In China, in particular, many incense burners were made out of ceramic, often copying ancient censer forms made from bronze that were used in burial rituals (**ill. 2**). Ash was poured inside these vessels to create a soft ground for the incense sticks. Such vessels were also used by the Chinese in Confucian and Daoist rituals.

Closed censers with smoke holes in the upper section were also common in East Asia. In Korea, in particular, censers appeared in the form of birds, animals, and mythical creatures, with holes in the creatures' mouths from which the smoke issued (**ill. 3**). Another type of incense burner that was often made in ceramic was a rectangular block with several holes in the top for the sticks of incense. This type of censer was often decorated with Buddhist symbols such as lotuses (48) or lions (53).

In China, Korea and Japan around the middle of the first millennium AD, small, closed censers with a single long handle were used. These portable incense burners were filled with incense and carried to the altar where they were placed (**ill. 4**). To disperse the sweet-smelling smoke, lumps of incense were sometimes placed inside perforated metal balls which were suspended from the ceilings of Buddhist temples and swung in the breeze or as people passed by. These incense balls were, like many other metalwork censers, often decorated with incised or inlaid designs of lotuses or other Buddhist motifs.

xianglu
 (Chinese)
goro
 (Japanese)
hyangnyo
 (Korean)

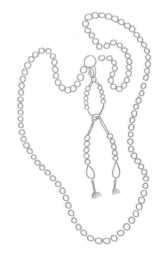

1 A string of Buddhist prayer beads, Japan (above)

2 Japanese priest with prayer beads, hand coloured woodblock print, Japan, 18th century (left)

3 Rosary of skulls, painting, Tibet, 16th century (below)

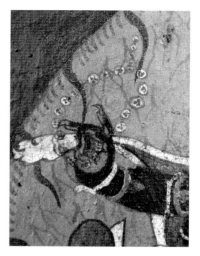

Symbolism and Function

Prayer beads, or rosaries, were probably introduced into Buddhism from Hinduism. They are used primarily in the esoteric Buddhist rituals of Tibet and Japan and are worn by priests and devotees alike. They are also the attributes of certain deities, most commonly the compassionate bodhisattva, Avalokiteshvara (8). Traditionally, Buddhist rosaries have 108 beads, representing the 108 human passions that Avalokiteshvara is believed to have assumed when telling the beads. It is also said that this number enabled worshippers to repeat the sacred name of the Buddha one hundred times, the extra beads allowing for any omissions made through absent-mindedness in counting or for the loss or breakage of beads.

Before being knotted, the string is passed through a large central bead and two smaller beads. These three additional beads keep the rest in place and indicate the completion of a cycle of telling. They are also said to symbolize the three jewels of Buddhism, the Buddha, the dharma (his teachings), and the sangha (the monastic order). The hidden string that passes through the beads symbolizes the penetrating power of all of the Buddhas (**ill. 1**).

Representations

Some rosaries are smaller, but the number of beads is generally divisible by three, for example, 21, 42, or 54 beads. Many Chinese rosaries have only 18 beads, one for each of the 18 lohans, or arhats (27). The beads are made from a variety of materials, most commonly wood, including sandalwood or sacred wood from the bodhi tree. More expensive rosaries are made of precious and semi-precious stones, including pearls, rubies, crystal, amber, coral, or jade, or precious metals such as gold. They can even be made of animal bone or seeds. The string is usually made of silk, but is sometimes made of human hair.

Prayer beads, or rosaries, are worn as bracelets, usually by followers of the Japanese and Tibetan esoteric schools of Buddhism. However, priests often carry longer strings of beads as necklaces. They use these beads to enable them to keep track of the numbers of prayers and incantations they make to the deities during prayers and meditational exercizes. Many paintings of important Buddhist priests or patriarchs show them seated on a platform wearing robes and fingering rosaries (**ill. 2**). Very large rosaries are also sometimes used in rituals to particular deities. For example, a ritual is held every summer in Kyoto in which children sit in a circle and pass round a large rosary to invoke the protection of the bodhisattva Kshitigarbha (11), guardian of children in Japan.

Rosaries are also the attributes of certain deities. Avalokiteshvara is often depicted holding a lotus (48), a water sprinkler (59) and a rosary of 108 beads, representing the bodhisattva's wish to help believers conquer the 108 passions and attain enlightenment. The compassionate Buddha Amitabha (6) is also sometimes depicted holding a rosary. Wrathful deities are sometimes shown holding rosaries made of skulls (**ill. 3**).

1 Buddhist monk, Doi Sothep, Thailand (above)

2 Priest's robe or kesa, brocaded silk, Japan, 19th century (below)

3 Tibetan monks wearing elaborate robes and hats, painting (detail) on cloth, Tibet, 18th century (right)

4 Five-part crown, Tibet or Nepal (below right)

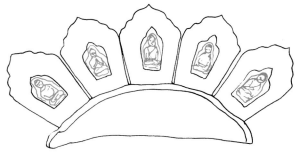

Symbolism and Function

The clothing worn by the monks and priests of the various schools of Buddhism varies greatly, from the simple saffron robes of the monks of Thailand and Sri Lanka to the highly elaborate robes and headdresses of the lamas of Tibet. The colours and forms of the robes and hats they wear are usually symbolic of some aspect of the Buddha's life and teachings or of the Buddhist cosmos.

Main Representations

The Historical Buddha (1) is believed to have worn a humble monk's robe made up of patched pieces of donated cloth throughout his life as an enlightened being. He is depicted in painting and sculpture with such a robe draped over his body, often leaving his right shoulder bare. Similarly, the monks of the Southern Theravada tradition of Sri Lanka and Southeast Asia wear plain saffron robes, partly in emulation of the Buddha's humble garb, but also to represent their own detachment from the material world during their pursuit of spiritual enlightenment (**ill. 1**) In some cases, they dress statues of the Buddha in similar saffron robes.

In the Buddhist traditions of the Northern Schools, the clothing of monks varies considerably, often due to geography and climate. In paintings, the founders of many East Asian Buddhist sects are often depicted in painting wearing beautifully embroidered and brocaded silk robes. However, the monks of many of the schools of China, Korea and Japan generally wear more austere grey or black robes, with a simple cloth collar suspended around their necks. In Japan, a type of prayer robe known as a kesa, was worn over the regular robes. Kesa were usually patched together with scraps of fine silk brocade in imitation of the Buddha's patchwork robes. Their geometric patterns, like those of painted mandalas, have been said to symbolize the universe (**ill. 2**).

The most elaborate Buddhist robes are generally found in the Himalayan region, within the context of Vajrayana Buddhist rituals. As with much of the Buddhist art of this region, the robes and hats of Buddhist monks and lamas are often extremely colourful, the colours varying according to the particular sect (**ill. 3**). The monks of the various sects of Tibetan Buddhism can often be identified by the colour of their hats; for example, monks of the Gelukpa order, to which the Dalai Lama belongs, wear yellow pointed hats. During particular Vajrayana Buddhist ceremonies, including exorcisms, the lamas wear large helmet-like headdresses with crescent-shaped peaks.

In other ceremonies, including initiation ceremonies, lamas wear crowns made up of five sections, each containing one of the Five Transcendental Buddhas or the Sanskrit seed syllables which represent their essence (**ill. 4**). While wearing such crowns, the monk or priest summons up a particular deity, who may be depicted in a painting wearing a similar five-part crown.

1 Prayer wheel, wood, bronze, and cloth tassel, Tibet, 19th century (left)

2 Prayer wheel, Tibet (right)

Symbolism and Function

The prayer wheel is used by Buddhist practitioners particularly in the Himalayan religion, where it provides a simple way for devotees to symbolically recite sacred texts or invoke particular deities without actually reading the sutras. A prayer wheel consists of a closed metal cylinder with a long metal or wooden handle piercing its axis. The cylinder contains a text written or printed on paper or animal skin, usually sutras or invocations to particular deities, either sacred charms known as dharani or secret formulas known as mantra relating to the deities. The most common of these mantras is 'Om mani padme hum', or 'Praise to the Jewel in the Lotus', a mantra to the compassionate bodhisattva Avalokiteshvara (8). Suspended from the outside of the cylinder is a chain with a weight on its end, which helps the wheel to turn as the user rotates his or her wrist.

Prayer wheels are most often used by Vajrayana Buddhists of Tibet and Nepal. Hand-held prayer wheels are carried by pilgrims and other devotees and are turned during devotional activities. Each turn of the wheel is believed to have as much merit as actually reading or reciting the text inside. The belief in the effectiveness of turning a prayer wheel derives from the Buddhist belief in the power of sound and the formulas to which deities were subject. To many Buddhists, particularly in Tibet, it also represents the Wheel of the Law (42) and the turning of the wheel symbolizes the first teaching of the Buddha, when he set the Wheel of the Law in motion. Such a device is also useful for illiterate members of the lay Buddhist community, since they can read the prayer symbolically by turning the wheel.

Features and Representations

Prayer wheels are generally made out of repoussé metal, usually gilded bronze. The wheel itself is often supported on a handle made of wood or a precious metal (**ill. 1**). Around the outside of the cylinder are inscriptions, often written in Sanskrit, as well as Buddhist auspicious symbols (**ill. 2**). This outer section can usually be removed to allow the insertion of the sacred text into the cylinder. The uppermost point of the prayer wheel is often in the form of a lotus bud.

Larger prayer wheels can also be found at the gates of monasteries and temples or around stupas. The devotee turns the prayer wheel before passing through the gates. Some wheels are so large that they are enclosed in small buildings and are turned using a mill that is powered by flowing water.

hkor-brten,
khorten
(*Tibetan*)

1 The five geometric forms of the stupa, Japan (below left)

2 The Tabotap Pagoda, stone, Pulguksa, Kyongju, Korea, 8th century (left)

3 The pagoda at Kiyomizu temple, wood, Kyoto, Japan (below right)

4 Stupa, gilded bronze, Nepal, 17th century (below centre)

Symbolism and Function

Stupas are essentially containers for relics of the Historical Buddha or important Buddhist teachers or saints. They derive from ancient Indian burial mounds that marked the graves of religious or political leaders and reminded the living of their power. After the death of Shakyamuni (1), they were incorporated into Buddhism as containers of the relics of the Buddha and other holy figures, and as reminders of his enlightenment and symbols of his physical body and his teachings. As the stupa resembles a hill, it has also been thought to represent Mount Meru, the sacred mountain (52) at the centre of the Buddhist universe. A pole that passes through the centre of the structure linking the top of the stupa to the relics beneath serves as an axis mundi, or cosmic pillar, connecting heaven and earth.

Followers of esoteric schools believe that the stupa also represents the cosmos. It is constructed of five geometric forms representing each of the elements (**ill. 1**). The square base represents matter, while the circle above it represents knowledge. Next, the triangle symbolizes the spirit, and the semi-circle represents the Buddhist Law. Crowning the construct is a flaming jewel symbolizing the supreme Principle.

Representations

In early Buddhist practice in India, large stone stupas containing Buddhist relics were the most important objects of worship. Devotees walked clockwise around them as a devotional act. The most celebrated example is the Great Stupa at Sanchi (75), a large mound surrounded by carved stone gates and topped by three small umbrella forms. Similar stupas were also featured in Indian Buddhist stone relief carvings, in which worshippers were depicted praying to stupas. In the Theravada cultures of Sri Lanka and Southeast Asia, these monuments to the Historical Buddha and his teachings are primary objects of worship. In most cases, the stupa has retained its original form, with a square base, round central section, and umbrella forms at the top. However, in Thai and Burmese stupas in particular, the round section was reduced, resulting in slender, triangular forms, often covered in gold.

In China, Korea, then Japan, the stupa underwent a fascinating transformation, evolving into pagodas with several storeys. These wood, brick or stone structures also house holy relics and have a pole connecting the relics to the top of the structure. The small umbrella forms are still at the very top, but in most cases, the round section of the original form has vanished. In Korea, many pagodas were architectural marvels made of stone, such as the Tabotap pagoda at the Pulguksa temple (**ill. 2**). In Japan, numerous wooden pagodas have odd numbers of graceful eaves and can be entered (**ill. 3**).

In many Buddhist cultures, smaller stupas or pagodas are used for personal worship, usually from wood, stone or bronze (**ill. 4**). Certain deities are depicted with small stupas as their attributes. Maitreya (3), the Buddha of the Future, often wears a small stupa in his headdress, while Vaishravana (19), the Guardian King of the North, holds one in his left hand.

shuaidupo, ta
  (Chinese)
sotoba, to
  (Japanese)
mchod-rten,
  chorten
  (Tibetan)
chedi (Thai)

1 Altar to the Buddha, Wat Sri Chum, Sukhothai, Thailand (left)

2 Household shrine, Japan (above)

3 Buddhist shrine in a Thai restaurant, Los Angeles (below)

Symbolism and Function

Most Buddhists who venerate a particular Buddha, bodhisattva or other deity worship at a temple in a main hall that houses the principal figure of the sect to which the temple belongs. In front of the main figure of worship, most typically a seated or standing Buddha or bodhisattva, is an altar on which are placed offerings to the image, including flowers, incense and other objects, depending on the sect. The presiding priest of the temple conducts prayers and rituals in front of the altar, often before a large congregation. In many Buddhist homes, smaller altars or shrines are placed in the corner or in a quiet room where family members can worship their personal deities. Like the priest in a temple, the lay worshipper offers flowers, food, candles and incense to the deity on the household altar. The altar or the household shrine is, therefore, an important place in Buddhist worship, since it is where the worshipper makes a connection with the object of worship. As such, it is treated with the utmost reverence.

Representations

The altars of Buddhist temples vary depending on the size, importance, wealth and sect of the particular temple. In general, the altars in front of images of the Buddha in the Theravada temples of Sri Lanka and Southeast Asia are relatively simple, as the manner of worship in the Southern traditions is relatively simple. An incense burner (61) and flowers provide the main offerings to images of the Buddha (**ill. 1**).

In contrast, many of the altars in the esoteric Buddhist temples of Tibet, Nepal and Japan are adorned with vajras (55), bells (58), lamps and other objects. These objects are used by the presiding priest or lama in the rituals and prayers associated with the particular deity and sect. Behind or at either side of the altar, paintings on cloth of deities or mandalas are often hung. In Tibet, butter lamps are also kept lit around the altar, and small lidded metal cups are filled with water. Some of the altars of Vajrayana Buddhist temples in Tibet and Nepal have an area behind them reserved for priests.

In homes, altars appear in many materials and sizes, depending largely on the wealth and level of devotion of the household. In East Asia, portable wooden shrines resembling cupboards with two side doors that open outwards are a common form of household altar (**ill. 2**). Often decorated with gold, lacquer and other precious materials, they hold small wooden or bronze images of Buddhas and bodhisattvas. In many Buddhist households, during the eighth lunar month, the souls of deceased family members are believed to return home, and living family members place offerings of food and drink at household altars as an offering to these spirits. They also offer prayers for the peaceful repose of their ancestors' souls. In many Buddhist cultures, altars are also placed in a corner in shops, restaurants and other businesses as a prayer for protection and good fortune (**ill. 3**).

1 Sanskrit characters on a porcelain bowl, China, 17th century (far left)

2 The Sanskrit letter 'A' (left)

3 The Seed Mandala of the Diamond World, hand coloured woodblock print, Japan, 17th century (above)

Symbolism and Function

Many of the Buddhist sutras, or sacred texts, were originally written in Sanskrit, an ancient Indian language that belongs to the Indic group of Indo-European languages and is now written in the Devanagari script. The earliest form of the language, Vedic Sanskrit, was spoken for about one thousand years from *c.* 1800 BC and is the language in which the sacred Hindu texts, the *Vedas* and the *Upanishads*, were written. Classical Sanskrit, the form in which the *Ramayana* and *Mahabharata* were written, flourished from *c.* 500 BC to AD 1000, and is the form in which the Mahayana and Vajrayana Buddhist texts were written. The sacred texts of Theravada Buddhism are written in Pali, another Indic language closely related to Sanskrit.

In the Buddhist context, Sanskrit was not confined to sacred scriptures, but was also incorporated into paintings, ritual objects and many decorative arts. In many cases, an inscription written in Sanskrit characters accompanies the image of a deity. This inscription may be the Sanskrit name of the deity or it may represent a particular prayer or mantra (sacred formula) associated with the deity. The most well-known mantra, 'Om mani padme hum', or 'Praise to the jewel in the lotus', is associated with Avalokiteshvara (8) and may accompany images of this bodhisattva, adding spiritual power to the image.

Representations

Sanskrit inscriptions often appear on Buddhist ritual objects from countries other than India, where the language originated. In particular, objects from within the Himalayan Buddhist tradition often bear Sanskrit inscriptions. In cultures as distant as China and Japan, Sanskrit characters often embellish bowls, water containers, and other ritual vessels, indicating the sacred function of the container in Buddhist rituals (**ill. 1**).

In the more esoteric forms of Buddhism found in Tibet and Japan, single Sanskrit letters are also used alone to represent particular deities and their powers. Each Buddhist deity has a particular Sanskrit letter with which it is associated and which is believed to contain the essence, or seed, of the deity. These letters, known as the 'seed form' of the deity, are often used in place of figural representations of the deities themselves. In some cases, a painting might depict a Sanskrit character in the place of a Buddha, seated on a lotus throne. The most common example of this is the character 'A', the most powerful of the seeds, which symbolizes all beginnings and represents the Cosmic Buddha, Vairochana (4) (**ill. 2**).

The seed characters of the various Buddhas, bodhisattvas and other deities also replace the figural forms in elaborate mandalas (73), in particular Japanese Shingon Buddhist mandalas representing the dual worlds. In these mandalas, the seed characters are depicted on lotuses and arranged in hierarchical order (**ill. 3**). In the Mandala of the Diamond World, in place of the principal Buddha, the Cosmic Buddha Vairochana, in the top centre square is the Sanskrit character 'A' sitting on a large lotus throne.

大般若波羅蜜多經卷第百四
初分讚般若品第卅二之三
三藏法師玄奘奉　詔譯

復次世尊菩薩摩訶薩般若波羅蜜多於眼
男不住大不住小於色界眼識男及眼觸眼
觸為緣所生諸受亦不住大不住小於眼男
不住集不住散於色男乃至眼觸為緣所生
諸受亦不住集不住散於眼男不住有量不
住無量亦不住色男乃至眼觸男不住有量不
住有量不住色男乃至眼觸為緣所生諸受亦
於色男乃至眼觸男不住有力不住無力於色男
乃至眼觸為緣所生諸受亦不住有力不住
无力世尊我歸頂禮諸菩薩摩訶薩般若
波羅蜜多復次世尊菩薩摩訶薩般若
摩訶薩般若波羅蜜多於耳男及耳觸
於耳男耳識男及耳觸耳觸為緣所生諸受
亦不住大不住小於耳男不住大不住小於
聲男乃至耳觸為緣所生諸受亦不住大不
亦不住集於耳男乃至耳觸男不住有量不
住散於耳觸為緣所生諸受亦不住集於
至耳觸為緣所生諸受亦不住有力不住无
量於耳男乃至耳觸男不住有量不住

1 Leaf of the *Perfection of Wisdom Sutra*, ink, watercolours, gold on paper, Tibet, 11th–17th century (top)

2 Section of the *Perfection of Wisdom Sutra*, ink on paper mounted as a hand scroll, Japan, 8th century (above)

3 Section of the *Garland Sutra*, woodblock printed in the folding book format, China (left)

Symbolism and Function

The sutras are the sacred writings of Buddhism, and are one of the Tripitaka, or 'three baskets', the three major divisions of the Buddhist canon of scripture. The word *sutra* comes from the Sanskrit root meaning 'to sew', so a sutra is a thread of discourse or teachings. For centuries, sutras have been studied and recited in order to attain an understanding of the Buddhist Way, and copied or commissioned as an act of merit. There are hundreds of sutras all emphasizing different aspects of the teachings of the Historical Buddha (1) or explaining various paths to enlightenment. None was written by the Buddha himself, but were compiled by followers of his disciples centuries after his death. Different Buddhist sects emphasize the teachings of different sutras. Among the most widely used sutras in the Mahayana traditions are the *Perfection of Wisdom Sutra* (Sanskrit: *Prajnaparamita Sutra*) and the *Lotus Sutra* (Sanskrit: *Saddharma Pundarika*). In general, sutras were originally written in Sanskrit in the Northern traditions, or in Pali in the Southern traditions, and have been translated into the languages of the various Buddhist cultures. However, certain sutras, which do not exist in Sanskrit or Pali versions, may have originated outside India.

Over the centuries, sutras have been produced in many formats, depending on available materials. In most cultures, they are handwritten in ink on paper, or in some cases on palm leaves. In East Asia, the urge to disseminate Buddhist teachings to a wide audience gave rise to woodblock printing and later, movable type printing.

Loose-leaf Manuscript

In India, Nepal and areas of Southeast Asia, many religious scriptures were hand-written onto loose palm leaves and then tied together between two hard covers (**ill. 1**). The Tibetans were able to increase the size of these manuscripts by replacing the palm leaves with paper. Manuscript covers were usually made of wood and were often ornately decorated with gold or with paintings of the Buddhas, bodhisattvas, and deities. Often, images of the deities were painted on the individual pages.

Hand Scroll

In China, Korea, and Japan, many sutras were written onto sheets of paper that were attached together horizontally and then rolled up to form a hand scroll. The text was written from right to left, so the scroll was unrolled and read from right to left (**ill. 2**). These hand scrolls were often illustrated at the very front or end of the sutra, and in some scrolls, the illustrations came to dominate the text or replace it entirely.

Concertina Book

In East Asia, the folding book was a popular format for sutras. Sutras were either hand-written or printed onto several sheets of paper, which were then glued together and folded like a concertina. They were opened and read from right to left. The front and end sections were often decorated with scenes of Buddhist deities and paradises (**ill. 3**).

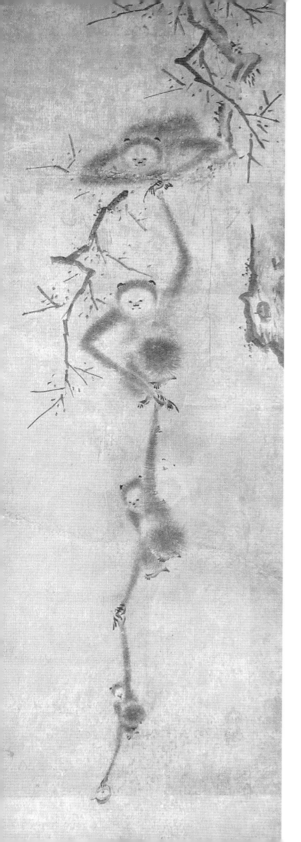

1 Chain of monkeys reaching for the reflection of the moon, ink on paper, Japan, 17th century (left)

2 Zen circle, Japan (above)

3 Zen calligraphy, 'to serve one's parents loyally', ink on paper, Japan, 19th century (below)

Symbolism and Function

Around the sixth century AD, the meditational (Sanskrit: dhyana) tradition of Mahayana Buddhism was transmitted by the Indian Buddhist monk Bodhidharma (28) to China, where it became known as *Chan*. Around the twelfth century AD, the tradition was transmitted to Japan, where it was known by its most common name, Zen. This tradition emphasizes cultivation of the self through meditation and direct experiences and eschews the texts, icons and imagery of other Northern Buddhist sects. However, it does not totally reject art. Artist monks in Chan temples in Southern China and later in the Zen Buddhist temples of Japan mastered the art of monochrome ink painting and calligraphy, skilfully using these art forms to express Zen principles such as simplicity and spontaneity. In both art forms, since the artist's brushstrokes cannot be corrected once on the paper, the artist's mind must be clear of distractions and focused on the moment.

Ink Paintings

Although Zen ink paintings often feature beautiful landscapes for the practitioner to meditate upon, many also depict human figures, in particular the Zen patriarchs of India, China, and Japan, at critical moments in their spiritual development. For example, Bodhidharma is shown in deep meditation in a cave, while the sixth patriarch of Zen, Hui Neng, is depicted at the moment of his enlightenment while chopping bamboo. Other Zen paintings illustrate Zen parables and conundrums, or *koan* in Japanese. One of the most popular didactic images is that of a monkey hanging from a tree and trying to grab at the reflection of the moon in a pool of water, an allegorical reference to the search for enlightenment (**ill. 1**). The foolish monkey does not realize that it cannot be attained easily. Another popular image is that of a young boy tugging at a stubborn ox, representing the challenge of controlling and then releasing one's true self in order to attain enlightenment. Also popular with Japanese Zen artists were paintings of the bullfrog who sits very still for long periods of time, an activity common to Zen practitioners. These paintings are all depicted with bold, spontaneous brushwork, and are often filled with humour.

Some of the most intriguing ink paintings depict a simple circle, which represents the entire universe in a single, perfect stroke (**ill. 2**). Though apparently simple, these images are difficult to paint successfully, as they must be painted with the right mind.

Calligraphy

The calligraphic messages of famous Zen masters were highly valued by their pupils and are some of the most remarkable Zen creations. These writings were often very short phrases, written with only a handful of Chinese characters, but loaded with spiritual meaning (**ill. 3**). For example, the phrase 'When you meet the Buddha on the road, kill him!' emphasizes the Zen disdain of concepts such as 'Buddha-hood' or 'enlightenment', since these concepts can obstruct direct experience of the world .

zenga,
zensho
(Japanese)

1 Wheel of the Six Realms of Rebirth, painting on silk, Tibet, 18th century (left)

2 Rooster, pig and snake representing attachment, ignorance and anger Tibet (below)

Symbolism and Function

The principal objective of Buddhists is to release the soul from the perpetual cycle of birth, death, and rebirth, known as samsara. In Buddhism, this release of the soul, or nirvana, is attained through the attainment of spiritual enlightenment, or an understanding of the true nature of all things. This concept originated in the Hindu philosophy that all beings are chained to this cycle, and that one's actions, or karma, determine the level of the rebirth of one's soul. Good deeds, or good karma, in one's present life lead to a higher rebirth, and immoral behaviour, or bad karma, leads to a lower rebirth. Similarly, one's present circumstances are the result of actions, or karma, in a previous existence and are almost impossible to alter.

In Buddhist teachings, there are Six Realms into which the soul can be reborn: 1) Deities, 2) Humans, 3) Beasts, 4) Hungry Ghosts, 5) Warlike Demons, or Ashuras (26), and 6) Hell. Of these six, the realm of the deities is the only one which is higher than rebirth as a human, but to be reborn as a deity only takes the soul one step closer to enlightenment; it is not an end in itself. The lowest, and most horrible rebirth is in one of the Buddhist Hells (71). Ideally, each rebirth should be higher than the previous level, in a progression towards eventual enlightenment.

Representations

Images of the six realms of rebirth are particularly common in the art of Vajrayana Buddhism, in particular in Tibetan paintings illustrating the Law of Causality. They are also found in the imagery of East Asia, particularly of Japan. In images of the Wheel of Birth, Death, and Rebirth, also known as the Wheel of Becoming, the Six Realms are depicted within the spokes of a large wheel held by a fierce demon who represents impermanence (**ill. 1**). In the top centre, is the realm of the Deities, in which celestial figures are depicted dancing and flying around palaces in the clouds. Next, moving counter-clockwise, is the realm of Humans, showing scenes of daily life, including sickness and suffering. Following this is the realm of the Beasts, which includes all creatures who live on land, in the sea, and in the air. In the bottom centre is Hell, in which the souls of the condemned are shown being beaten or thrown into flames by demonic creatures with human bodies and animal heads. In the next realm, that of the Hungry Ghosts, are frightening creatures whose appetites can never be sated. They are usually depicted as thin naked figures with distended stomachs. In the final realm of the Warlike Demons, or Ashuras, figures are shown fighting and killing each other in a constant state of war.

At the very centre of this wheel are the harmful qualities of attachment, ignorance, and anger, represented by a mutually attached rooster, pig and snake respectively (**ill. 2**). In order to attain enlightenment and break free of the cycle of rebirth, one must transcend these three qualities. On the outer rim of the wheel are usually human figures who represent the chain of causality, a concept that explains how ignorance can lead to an accumulation of karma and a succession of rebirths. Ignorance is symbolized by the figure of a blind man.

gati (*Sanskrit*)
liufan (*Chinese*)
rokudo
　(*Japanese*)

1 Souls plunging into Hell, Japan (left)

2 Scene of Hell from the Wheel of Rebirth, woodblock print (detail), Japan, 19th century (below)

Naraka *(Sanskrit)*
jigoku *(Japanese)*
Diyu *(Chinese)*

Symbolism and Function

In Buddhist cosmology, Hell is the lowest of the Six Realms (70) of samsara, the never-ending cycle of rebirth. If a believer lives a wicked life, his karma may cause him to be reborn in Hell. According to certain Buddhist texts, there are a total of eighteen different hells, which are arranged in layers in the Buddhist cosmos, with the most horrible in the lowest sections. A person is reborn into a particular hell for a certain amount of time, sometimes eternity, depending on the nature of his misdeeds or crimes. In East Asian Buddhist texts, the Hell of Burning Excrement and the Hell of Knives are particularly gruesome fates awaiting the condemned. Images of the horrors of Hell were used by Buddhist priests in East Asia in particular as a means of discouraging wicked and immoral behaviour among the lay Buddhist population.

According to some Buddhist traditions, particularly in East Asia, the condemned soul is brought up before Yama (15), the King of Hell, or the Ten Kings of Hell, to hear his sentence before descending into hell. Once in hell, it is generally believed that a soul cannot be saved and will exist there for eternity. However, in certain Buddhist traditions, it is believed that relatives of the damned can petition and pray for that soul to be released from Hell. In China, Korea and Japan, it is believed that the compassionate bodhisattva Kshitigarbha (11) has the power to descend to the hells and save souls.

Representations

Scenes of the tortures of Buddhist hells are some of the most gruesome images in Buddhist art. In some representations, the souls of the damned, often depicted in the form of naked human beings, are shown plunging head first into Hell. There, they are met by demonic creatures with human bodies and animal heads who are standing ready to impale them with spears or force them into a pit of flames (**ill. 1**). Such images were usually painted or printed and were shown as illustrations by monks as they described the horrors of Hell to the lay population. Some of the most remarkable images of this type are the hand scrolls depicting scenes of Hell produced in Japan in the twelfth and thirteenth centuries.

Scenes of the Buddhist hells are most commonly seen in painted or printed images of the Six Realms of Rebirth, in which each realm is depicted within the spokes of a large Wheel of Life, Death and Rebirth. Scenes of hell usually appear at the bottom section of the wheel since hell is the lowest, and most awful, level of rebirth in the cycle. In some Chinese and Japanese examples, Yama, the King of Hell, is shown as a fearsome official handing out sentences and punishments to terrified figures from behind a huge desk (**ill. 2**). Demonic figures with horses' or cows' heads then drag the souls, off to meet their fate.

1 Amitabha and Attendants, Tibet (below right)

2 The Western Paradise of Amitabha, embroidered silk, Japan/China, 20th century (right)

3 The Byodoin Temple, Uji, Japan, 1052–53 (below)

Symbolism and Function

According to Buddhist sutras, each of the Buddhas, bodhisattvas, and certain other deities inhabits a specific paradise or Pure Land, a perfected world that is either far away beyond our realm or somewhere on earth. For example, the Healing Buddha Bhaishajyaguru (2) resides in the Lapis Lazuli Paradise and Akshobhya (5) resides in Abhirati, both of which are located in the East. Amitabha (6) inhabits the Western Pure Land, or Western Paradise known as Sukhavati. These realms are considered to be in far away universes, but the souls of the faithful can be transported there after death and reborn there. These paradises are not considered the final goal of the Buddhist devotee, but simply a step on the path towards enlightenment. Once reborn in these paradises, souls receive the assistance of the presiding Buddha or other being in their quest for enlightenment.

For many worshippers, the vision of these glorious paradises became more appealing than the concept of extinction, or nirvana itself. In Tibet, devotees to the various Buddhas chant magical mantras, such as 'Om mani padme hum', 'Praise to the jewel in the lotus', or turn prayer wheels (64) bearing the same mantra, believing that these sacred sounds will transport their souls to one of the pure lands. In Japan, devotees to Amitabha chant 'Namu Amida Butsu', 'Praise to Amitabha Buddha', in the hope of being reborn in his paradise.

In our earthly realm are several other paradises, such as the Potalaka Paradise of Avalokiteshvara (8) and Tara (9) located somewhere to the south of India, and the Copper Mountain Paradise of the Tibetan guru, Padmasambhava (29) believed to be situated southwest of India, possibly as far away as Africa. Devotees can visit these pure lands in their dreams and move closer to enlightenment.

Representations

The most common Buddhist paradise scenes are Tibetan or Japanese images of Amitabha in his Western Paradise. In Tibetan images, Amitabha is crowned and bejeweled, not unlike a bodhisattva. He sits in his palace, which is generally modelled after Chinese palace and temple architecture, with a central building and wings. At his side are the bodhisattvas, Avalokiteshvara and Mahastamaprapta, and all around him are celestial figures providing entertainment (**ill. 1**). In front of the celestial group is a lotus pond, and on some of the lotuses one can see babies emerging from the lotuses, representing souls newly born into the paradise. The best-known Japanese image of Amitabha's paradise is the Taima Mandara, an eighth century woven depiction of this paradise that was housed in the Taima temple in Nara (**ill. 2**).

Three dimensional recreations of these paradises also exist. Amitabha's paradise, for example, was recreated in eleventh century Japan at the Byodoin temple complex in Uji, near Kyoto by an aristocratic devotee. The building houses a large gilded image of Amitabha and in front of it is a pond full of lotuses (**ill. 3**). The official Tibetan residence of the Dalai Lama, known as the Potala Palace (83), was named after Avalokiteshvara's paradise, Potalaka, by the Great Fifth Dalai Lama.

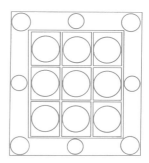

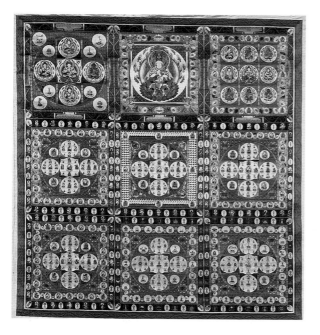

1 Tibetan monks making sand mandala (above left)

2 The three-dimensional Mandala of the Peaceful and Wrathful Deities of the one hundred Buddha Families (Tibetan: Shi-tro Mandala), wood, plaster, fibreglass, polychrome, gilding, Tibet/USA 2000 (left)

3 Diagram of centre of one type of mandala (above)

4 Diamond and 5 Womb World Mandalas, Japan, 2000 (below left and right respectively)

Symbolism and Function

A mandala is a type of cosmological diagram used by Hindus, Jains, and Buddhists as a visualization device to help practitioners in their search for spiritual enlightenment. The Sanskrit word mandala means a sacred centre ('la') that has been set apart or adorned ('mand'). For Mahayana and Vajrayana Buddhists, a mandala is a model or a map of a perfected universe in which a deity or many deities reside.

These elaborate diagrams are believed to represent the sacred abodes or universes of single Buddhas, bodhisattvas, or other deities, or even of groups of deities. Practitioners of Tibetan Vajrayana Buddhism and of Japanese esoteric Buddhism use mandalas to attempt to attain the type of enlightenment associated with particular deities. They concentrate on the mandala of a particular deity, striving to visualize every detail of the architecture and environment of the mandala. With enough effort and concentration, they are able to visualize themselves within the realm of the deity. Once inside the perfected universe of the deity, the practitioner can move a step closer towards spiritual enlightenment.

Representations

Most Buddhist mandalas are created and used by the Vajrayana Buddhists of Tibet and Nepal, but practitioners of the Japanese Shingon sect of esoteric Buddhism also use them as visualization devices. In Tibetan Buddhism, there are hundreds of different mandalas for the numerous deities of the Vajrayana Buddhist pantheon. Although mandalas can be created in many different forms, most mandalas are painted, printed, or embroidered geometrical patterns, often resembling the floor plan of a palace, with central and outer halls and four main gates. A typical Tibetan mandala is painted in mineral pigments on a cloth ground, although mandalas made of sand are also traditional (**ill. 1**). These are carefully constructed over several weeks and then brushed or blown away in a gesture that acknowledges the impermanence of existence. In Tibet, three-dimensional mandalas resembling palaces built on mountains are also constructed, but these are relatively rare (**ill. 2**).

In most Tibetan mandalas, the main deity or group of deities are shown in the very central section of the mandala surrounded by symmetrically arranged sections, or rooms (**ill. 3**), containing lesser deities and encircled by lotuses (48), vajras (55), and flames. Colour is also highly symbolic in these mandalas, with each direction being represented by a separate colour: green for north, white for east, yellow for south, and red for west.

In Japanese Shingon Buddhism, the most important are the Mandalas of the Two Worlds: the Diamond/Thunderbolt World (Sanskrit: Vajradhatu) and the Womb World, (Sanskrit: Garbhadhatu) which represent the dual aspects (male/female, compassion/wisdom, day/night, etc.) of the universe. In this pair of mandalas, the central figures are representations of the Cosmic Buddha Vairochana (4) in his active and passive aspects. The principal figures in these mandalas are surrounded by lesser deities, all seated on lotus thrones (36) and arranged in a hierarchical order (**ill. 4, 5**).

mandara
 (Japanese)
mandala (Korean)
mandala (Tibetan)

1 Tibetan monks at Bodh Gaya (below)

2 Shakyamuni attaining enlightenment under the bodhi tree, Sri Lanka (left)

3 Model of Bodh Gaya, schist, India, 11th–12th century (far left)

Bodh Gaya in Bihar in northeastern India is the most sacred of all Buddhist sites since it is where the Buddha attained enlightenment under a pipal tree (*ficus religiosa*). The tree, often known as the bodhi tree, or tree of enlightenment, is at the centre of the Bodh Gaya complex. After the Buddha's death, cuttings of the original bodhi tree were sent to holy sites around the country. In the third century BC, a cutting was taken to Anuradhapura in Sri Lanka, where it grew into a huge tree. In the late nineteenth century, a cutting of this tree was brought by the British back to Bodh Gaya and planted where the original tree once stood. Beside it is the Mahabodhi (or 'Great Enlightenment') Temple and all around are buildings and trees associated with the Buddha's enlightenment. Although Buddhism lost favour in India in the second millennium, the site has been a major destination for Buddhist pilgrims for over 2,000 years (**ill. 1**).

Historical Background

According to tradition, Siddartha Gautama, or Shakyamuni (1), arrived in Bodh Gaya in around 590 BC. Intent on attaining enlightenment, he sat under a pipal tree to meditate (**ill. 2**). After forty-nine days of meditation, he achieved enlightenment, and spent the following seven weeks in Bodh Ghaya deliberating how to pass on his understanding to others. In c. 250 BC, the Mauryan Emperor Ashoka, a Buddhist convert, erected a temple commemorating the Buddha's enlightenment at Bodh Ghaya. It did not survive, but the present structure was erected on the same site in the second century AD and repaired at various points in its history. In 637 AD, when the Chinese pilgrim Xuanzang (30) visited the holy site, he noted monasteries, stupas (65) and other buildings built by kings and noble figures to preserve the memory of the Buddha over the centuries. Many elements of the temple complex have been repaired by Burmese Buddhists, first in the eleventh century, and again by devout Burmese Buddhist rulers in the early nineteenth century, so there are many Burmese stylistic elements in the sculpture and architecture of the buildings. Restoration work was completed in the late nineteenth century by the British under General Alexander Cunningham.

Main Features

The most notable element of the Bodh Gaya temple complex is the towering Mahabodhi temple, a stone structure with a central shikhara (**ill. 3**). It rises up like a narrow pyramid and ends in the form of a Burmese-style stupa. At the four sides of the shikhara are entrances to the temple and at the corners are smaller shikharas, probably added later to conform to Hindu temple design. The facades of the central and four corner towers are covered with niches that were originally filled with statues of Buddhist figures relating to the four directions. These have mostly been replaced by an assortment of statues recovered during restoration. Next to the temple is the bodhi tree surrounded by a stone throne, known as the Diamond Throne, which marks the spot where the Buddha sat. Monks and pilgrims circumambulate the tree and place offerings before it or on the throne around the tree.

1 Elevation of Great Stupa at
Sanchi (below)

2 The Great Stupa and Gate,
Sanchi (above)

3 Gate, or torana, at Sanchi (left)

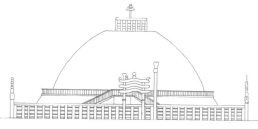

Sanchi, with its large, stone-covered stupa (65), is the oldest and arguably the most important of all surviving Buddhist monuments. Forty miles from the city of Bhopal, the site of Sanchi dates to the third century BC and the rule of Emperor Ashoka. The site is best known for its burial mound, known as the Great Stupa, a large dome surrounded by a stone railing and four stone gates (**ill. 1**). These gates, which were added at a later date, feature some of the earliest and most beautiful examples of Buddhist sculpture. The stupa is believed to contain relics of the Historical Buddha (1), and is still venerated as a holy space today. Worshippers enter through the eastern gate and ascend steps on the stupa platform to a walkway where they circumambulate the dome in a clockwise direction.

Historical Background

The Mauryan Emperor Ashoka's passionate dedication to the Buddha's teachings led to Buddhism's position as a world religion and the dominant one of Asia. After a battle in which thousands perished, Ashoka was overcome with regret and abhorrence for violence, and converted to Buddhism. He saw himself as a virtuous chakravartin, a powerful, almost divine ruler whose role on earth paralleled that of the Buddha in the spiritual realm. As such, Ashoka attempted to unite the empire under the Buddhist Law, constructing 84,000 stupas throughout India, each containing Buddhist relics, and erecting numerous pillars inscribed with edicts proclaiming the virtues of the Buddhism. At Sanchi, the site of an early monastery, Ashoka built a stupa 60 feet in diameter and 25 feet high surrounded by wooden railings. In the mid-second century BC, the stupa was doubled in size and the wooden railings replaced by stone railings 9 feet high. At the end of the first century BC, the stupa was renovated. Four gates, or toranas, were added; they were completed in the first century AD.

Main Features

The Great Stupa is at once a sacred burial mound containing Buddhist relics, a symbol of the Buddha's enlightenment, and a model of the Buddhist cosmos (**ill. 1**). The stupa consists of a solid dome made of mud, bricks and mortar and contains holy relics. Through the centre of the dome, a pillar extends upwards and above the top of the dome, symbolizing the pivot of the universe, the axis mundi. It is topped by three circular disks, representing the Three Jewels (49), or triratna, of Buddhism: the Buddha, the dharma (teachings), and the sangha (monastic order). The stupa is surrounded by a stone railing, or harmika, and at the cardinal points are four stone toranas, each with three cross beams (**ill. 2**). These beams were all elaborately carved with symbols such as trees (51), lotuses (48), stupas, wheels (47) and empty thrones (36), all representing Shakyamuni and his teachings. Where the beams meet the pillars of the gates are elephants (53), lions, and dwarves, and side brackets are in the forms of voluptuous female deities, or yakshi (26) (**ill. 3**). The lower sections of the square pillars are carved with jataka tales, stories of the previous lives of the Buddha.

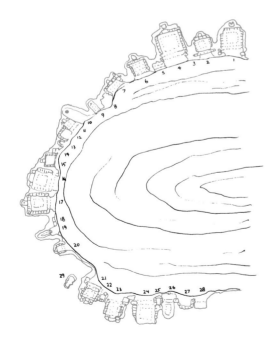

1 Plan of the Caves at Ajanta (below left)

2 Stupa with figure of seated Buddha, Cave 19, Ajanta (left)

3 Painted figure of Padmapani, Cave 1, Ajanta (below)

The Ajanta cave complex in the northwest Deccan region of India was cut out of a horseshoe shaped ravine between the second century BC and the seventh century AD. There are twenty-nine caves, a mixture of Buddhist worship halls, or chaityas, and monasteries or viharas, where Buddhist monks lived and studied (**ill. 1**). These caves contain some of the earliest surviving examples of Indian painting and numerous outstanding sculpted images of Buddhist figures and scenes. Several of them date to the Gupta period (fourth to seventh centuries AD) and are some of the most refined Buddhist images created in India. Many of these images became the model for Buddhist imagery in other parts of Asia.

Historical Background

The caves of Ajanta are believed to have experienced two periods of activity, the first around the first century BC, the second during the Gupta period, during a 50 to 60 year period in the fifth and the sixth centuries AD. In the Gupta period, often considered the Classical Period of Indian arts, science, music and literature, many Buddhist and Hindu images were created by artists in north-central India. In the fifth century, some of the finest Buddhist paintings and sculptures were produced by Gupta artists, many of whom worked at the cave complex. Little information has survived about the patronage of the artistic works of these caves. Around the seventh century, due to the decreasing popularity of Buddhism in India, activity at Ajanta ceased. The caves were forgotten until 1817, when British soldiers rediscovered them while on a tiger hunt.

Main Features

The most complex elements of the Ajanta caves are the chaitya halls, where Buddhist monks worshipped. In these halls, the main object of worship was the stupa (65), which was carved out of the rock in the centre of the rounded end section to permit circumambulation. The Gupta period stupas feature elaborate carvings, including figures of the Buddha standing between pillars (**ill. 2**). All around the stupas are pillars and window-like niches featuring detailed carvings, which are reminiscent of wooden architecture. The walls of many of the chaitya halls and the viharas are lavishly decorated with paintings of Buddhas, bodhisattvas, and jataka tales, or scenes from the previous lives of the Buddha Shakyamuni (1). The surface of the wall was prepared first by applying a coating of clay mixed with cow dung, straw, and animal hair, then covered with a white lime plaster, onto which designs were painted in mineral pigments. One of the most notable of the Gupta period paintings is the image of the bodhisattva Padmapani, a form of Avalokiteshvara, painted on the wall to the right of a carved stone image of the Buddha in Cave 1 (**ill. 3**). The bodhisattva is drawn with an elegance that characterizes Gupta-style art. He stands holding a lotus in his right hand, his body swaying in the triple-bend, or tribangha pose. His face has a serene expression, as if focusing on something remote.

1 Great Stupa at Polonnaruwa (left)

2 Seated Buddha at Gal Vihara, Polonnaruwa, 12th century (above)

3 Dying Buddha and standing figure at Gal Vihara, Polonnaruwa, 12th century (below)

Polonnaruwa became the capital of Sri Lanka in the eighth century and from the twelfth century was the centre of the Theravada tradition of Buddhism in Sri Lanka. At the Gal Vihara temple in Polonnaruwa are several colossal stone images of the Buddha depicting significant moments of his life. These figures attest to the popularity of the Historical Buddha and his teachings among followers of the Theravada tradition, which gained strength under the Sinhalese Buddhist rulers of Sri Lanka.

Historical Background

Buddhism has been practised on the island of Sri Lanka for over 2,000 years and possibly from the time of the Buddha, who, according to legends, travelled there three times. In the second millennium, Theravada Buddhism flourished under the Sinhalese rulers of Sri Lanka, resulting in the construction of great monuments and the spread of Buddhism by Sri Lankan monks into Southeast Asia. In the twelfth century, under the rule of the Sinhalese King Parakramabahu (1153–86), some of Polonnaruwa's most remarkable Buddhist art and architecture was created. Parakramabahu built everything on a massive scale, including palaces, gardens, water tanks, and a number of Buddhist monasteries. At his northern monastery, Gal Vihara, he commissioned huge statues of the Historical Buddha (1), the only Buddha revered in the Theravada tradition, to be carved out of the rock face as a monument to the teachings of the Buddha.

Main Features

Polonnaruwa boasts a large stone stupa, built in a traditional manner, with a dome surmounted by a rectangular section and tapered spires, but with minimal surface decoration (**ill. 1**). The site is known primarily for its Buddha figures dating to the twelfth century. One figure from Gal Vihara is of the Buddha seated in the lotus position with hands in the meditation gesture (43) (**ill. 2**). He is simple and serene, echoing the direct, uncomplicated doctrine of the Theravada tradition, which stresses the solitary, individual path to enlightenment.

One of the most remarkable figures at Gal Vihara is of the Buddha lying on his right side at the moment of his death and final enlightenment (39) (**ill. 3**). The figure is c. 46 feet long, and the gentle face, the graceful curves of the body and the delicately carved robes that cling to his form are reminiscent of Indian Buddhist sculpture of the Gupta period (fourth to seventh centuries AD), particularly the stone reclining Buddha at Ajanta (76). This figure is all the more remarkable as it was carved out of a rock face, and the grain of the rock appears to be flowing gently along the length of the reclining Buddha's body. Next to the Buddha is a figure in monk's robes with his arms crossed. It may be Ananda, who continued teaching the Buddha's Way after the latter's death. His 23-foot standing figure is graceful and calm as he contemplates the true meaning of the Buddha's passing. Sockets cut into the rock behind these figures are evidence that each figure was originally enshrined within a separate wooden enclosure.

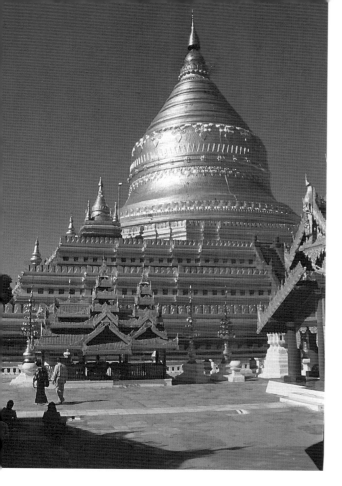

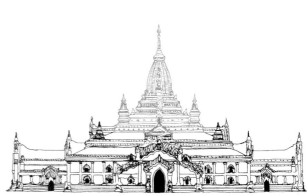

1 View of Pagan (below)

2 Ananda Temple, early 12th century, Pagan (above)

3 Shwedagon Pagoda, brick covered with gold, 11th century (left)

Pagan is an area in central Burma (Myanmar) measuring c. 25 square miles dotted with hundreds of temples and pagodas. The structures vary in size from small stone pagodas that stand crumbling in the fields to majestic temples, many of which were the first Buddhist structures to be created in a truly Burmese style (**ill. 1**). The village of Pagan was formerly the great capital of the kingdoms of Pagan, which enjoyed their golden age from the mid-eleventh to the end of the thirteenth century, at a time of transition from Mahayana to Theravada Buddhism. The temples and pagodas, all built during this golden age, mark the start of new Buddhist traditions in Burma.

Historical Background

The kingdoms of Pagan date back to the beginning of the Christian era, but the golden period of this culture is considered to have begun in 1057, with the conquest of the kingdom of Thaton by the Pagan ruler, Anawrahta, and ended in 1287, when Kublai Khan and his armies overran the area. Before King Anawrahta's rule, Hinduism and Mahayana Buddhism were prevalent in the Burmese kingdoms. When he ascended the throne, Anawrahta was persuaded by the King of Thaton to convert to the older Theravada Buddhism. When the King of Thaton refused to give Anawrahta some relics and texts that he requested, the latter invaded and conquered Thaton, bringing back to Pagan Buddhist relics and texts, as well as artists and architects. He and his successors embarked on a 200-year long programme of building of temples, stupas and libraries, which extend over the whole region. Palaces and other royal buildings were also part of the grandeur of the capital, but since they were built of wood, they have not endured.

Main Features

The Ananda Temple is one of the largest and best preserved of the Pagan temples (**ill. 2**) Named after one of the Buddha's chief disciples, this fine stone structure was built in 1105 and represents the infinite wisdom of the Buddha. The temple is constructed as a cross; in its centre is a cube, on each side of which is a standing Buddha. The structure rises upwards in terraces finishing in a peak in the form of a pointed stupa or shikhara. On the exterior walls are glazed tiles illustrating scenes from jataka tales, the stories of the past lives of the Buddha. Thatbinnyu Temple, built slightly later in the mid twelfth century, is the highest temple in Pagan and can be seen from all around the area.

Also notable at Pagan are the graceful pagodas, often made of brick and covered entirely with gold. Shwesandaw Pagoda was built in 1057, immediately after the conquest of Thaton. A graceful circular pagoda, the structure ascends in five square terraces, and two octagonal bases topped by a bell-like form. The colossal Shwedagon Pagoda, a more bulbous, bell-shaped structure built on a square stepped base and covered in gold, is often considered the prototype for later Burmese pagodas (**ill. 3**).

1 View of Wat Mahathat, Sukhothai (above)

2 Lotus bud finial on top of Wat Mahathat, Sukhothai (above left)

3 Seated Buddha, 13th or 14th century, Wat Mahathat, Sukhothai (below left)

4 Relief carvings of walking Buddhas, 13th or 14th century, Wat Mahathat, Sukhothai (below)

Sukhothai, meaning 'Rising of Happiness', was the first capital of the Thai people and flourished from the mid-thirteenth to the late fourteenth centuries. Located north of Bangkok, Sukhothai was constructed as a rectangular city surrounded by earthen walls. Its Buddhist temples and monuments, were constructed out of durable stone, while palaces and houses were built from wood and have not survived. The stone structures of Sukhothai, mostly stupas (65) and monuments, feature a variety of architectural styles from Buddhist sites from other cultures, enhancing the holy character of the city (**ill. 1**). The site borrows from the earlier architecture of the Mon people of the region, elements from Khmer architecture, and details from Sri Lankan Buddhist sites. However, it is also at Sukhothai where purely Thai architectural details, such as the lotus-bud finials on stupas, and sculptural styles such as the Walking Buddha (37) image, appeared for the first time.

Historical Background

The era of the Sukhothai Kingdom is considered the Golden Age of Thai civilization. The Sukhothai monarchy followed the teachings of Theravada Buddhism and patronized the construction of many temples, stupas and figures of the Buddha. The first Sukhothai ruler, King Intradit, began the building of the city of Sukhothai in the thirteenth century, possibly on the foundations of an earlier uncompleted Khmer city. After his death, his son, Ramkamhaeng (ruled c. 1275–c. 1315), and other succeeding rulers added to the city and restored earlier buildings. In the late fourteenth century, the southern kingdom of Ayudhaya conquered Sukhothai territory, reducing the city to the position of vassal state. By the sixteenth century, the city had fallen into ruin.

Main Features

Within the city of Sukhothai, the most important complex of Buddhist buildings are Wat Mahathat, the 'Great Relic Temple', a cluster of nearly 200 stupas, the bases of ten assembly halls and other temple structures. The principal structures of this complex are aligned along an east-west axis linking the rising and the setting sun. At the core of Wat Mahathat is a tall stupa crowned with a lotus-shaped finial, a detail that is unique to Thai Buddhist architecture (**ill. 2**). The stupa is surrounded by smaller towers, built out of brick or laterite (a clay-like material) and coated with stucco.

At Wat Mahathat and the other Buddhist sites in Sukhothai are many figures of the Buddha created out of brick or laterite covered in stucco (**ill. 3**). Many are of a monumental size, while others are more human in scale. These images feature the elegant, swaying bodies of the Sukhothai period, with clothes that seem to cling to their forms, and hair that ends in the shape of a rising flame at the top of their heads. Their faces are characterized by a gentle smile and strong, curved lines that represent the eyebrows but continue to form the long, prominent nose. Relief carvings of multiple figures of walking disciples, are also characteristic of this period (**ill. 4**).

1 The Bayon in Angkor Thom, stone, 13th century (above)

2 Plan of the Bayon, Angkor Thom (below)

3 Head of Avalokiteshvara at Angkor Thom, stone, 13th century (left)

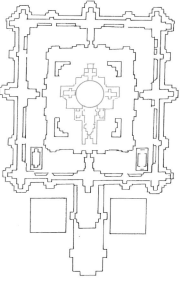

The temples of Angkor in Cambodia are some of the world's most magnificent architectural achievements. Built from the ninth to the thirteenth centuries, at the height of the power of the Khmer empire, the hundred or so temples are a mixture of Hindu and Buddhist architecture and imagery, reflecting the gradual shift in Khmer patronage from Hinduism to Buddhism in the eleventh and twelfth centuries. The ancient fortified city of Angkor Thom was the centre of Khmer power and its focal point was the Bayon, an impressive monument devoted to the bodhisattva Avalokiteshvara (8). To the south is the Hindu temple, Angkor Wat, built to honour Vishnu. Other temples are devoted to deified members of the Khmer ruling family.

Historical Background

The Khmer empire ruled over what is now Cambodia, parts of Thailand and Vietnam from the early ninth century to the fourteenth century. Their capital, Angkor, was considered by the Khmer rulers to be the centre of the universe. The rulers saw themselves as god-kings, or devaraja, an Indian concept that they embraced whole-heartedly, equating themselves to specific Hindu and Buddhist deities and building numerous monuments in their honour. King Jayavarman VII (ruled 1181–1219) was the greatest Khmer Buddhist monarch and was responsible for many of the impressive structures of the city, including the walled fortress of Angkor Thom and the Bayon within its walls. The power of the Khmers came to an end in the early fifteenth century when Thai armies attacked Angkor and other cities. At this time, Hinayana monks took over Angkor and turned it into a major centre for Buddhist pilgrimages. When the French first discovered this city in the 1860s, it was practically hidden in jungle vegetation. For the next century, French and local archaeologists cleared away much of the vegetation and began the restoration of many of the buildings.

Main Features

The most remarkable Buddhist structure at Angkor is the Bayon, a mountain-like temple within the walls of Angkor Thom. It is a complex arrangement on three levels, with 49 pyramidal towers rising up from the uppermost level, and five large towers in the centre (**ill. 1**). The largest central tower represents Mount Meru (52), the cosmic mountain at the centre of the Hindu and Buddhist universe. The structure is surrounded by a moat, representing the great cosmic ocean. Viewed from above, the structure resembles a Buddhist mandala (73), with Mount Meru in the centre and four gates at each of the cardinal directions (**ill. 2**). Such a temple mountain or mandala was not created as a site for group worship, but rather served as the residence of a god-king. Carved onto the sandstone walls of the towers are roughly 200 faces of Avalokiteshvara, looking out in all directions (**ill. 3**). These faces are said to be modelled on Jayavarman VII's own face and symbolize his role of god-king at the centre of the universe. Below, on the walls of the Bayon is an abundance of bas relief carvings, including scenes of everyday life.

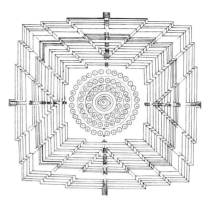

1 Plan of Borobodur (above)

2 Niches containing Buddhas on the middle levels of Borobodur (left)

3 Stupas containing Buddhas on the upper levels of Borobodur (below)

Borobodur, in central Java in Indonesia, is one of the largest and most complex monuments in the Buddhist world. Built around 800 AD, the solid, pyramid-like structure has been described as a funerary monument, a stupa (65), and a three-dimensional mandala (73). The building is formed of a square base, five lower square terraces and three upper round terraces, topped by a single large stupa. Many believe that the three sections of the structure represent levels of spiritual progress. Borobodur, which probably means 'monastery on the hill', has also been said to depict the history of the Buddhist faith, the lower levels representing the formative stages of the religion, the middle level representing the developments of the Mahayana schools, and the Buddhas and stupas at the top, the Vajrayana traditions.

Historical Background

The construction of Borobodur was started at the end of the eighth century AD when Java was under the rule of the Shailendra dynasty (730–930), who were followers of Mahayana Buddhism. At this time, while many of the cultures of Southeast Asia adopted Hinduism and Theravada Buddhism from India, Java maintained close cultural contact with northeastern India, a rich source of Mahayana Buddhist culture. Much of the Buddhist art and architecture of Java reflects this contact. According to early records, the colossal structure of Borobodur was originally begun around 770 as a Hindu monument, but by the end of the century, when the Shailendra had converted to Buddhism, it was modified to suit Buddhist needs. The mountain-like structure of Borobodur may have been built by Shailendra rulers not only as a monument to their Buddhist faith, but also to their dynasty, since the name Shailendra means 'Kings of the Mountains'. Around the year 1000, after the fall of the Shailendra, Borobodur fell into ruin. It was restored in 1907–11 and in the 1980s.

Main Features

Borobodur is remarkable for both its scale and its artistic detail. The square structure was built on top of a small hill and has sides over 360 feet long. When viewed from above, it closely resembles a Buddhist mandala with layers of concentric squares and circles (**ill. 1**). Its ten terraces can be divided into three levels, representing three realms of existence, or three levels of spiritual progress. The lowest level, a square base, represents kamadhatu, the earthly realm of passion and desire. The walls of this section are intricately carved with scenes of this world, scenes from the life of the Buddha, and jataka tales, stories from his previous lives. The middle layer of the five square terraces represents ruphadhatu, the celestial realm, and features niches containing 108 seated Buddha figures, facing in four directions (**ill. 2**). Above this are three round terraces with 72 stupas, each containing a single seated Buddha (**ill. 3**), and a single stupa at the very top. These four upper layers represent arupadhatu, the realm of formlessness and ultimate enlightenment. Practitioners climb the steps and walk clockwise around the structure, ascending towards symbolic enlightenment.

1 View of the valley of Bamiyan (below)

2 Standing Buddha at Bamiyan, stone, 136 feet high (left)

3 Standing Buddha at Bamiyan, stone, 186 feet high (above)

The valley of Bamiyan, Afghanistan, was home to one of the largest Buddhist centres in Central Asia during the first millennium. In the steep cliffs of the Koh-I-noor, or 'Hill of Saints', are c. 20,000 caves that were carved out of the cliff face, some large enough to function as Buddhist assembly halls, others serving as small individual residences (**ill. 1**). Sculpted from the cliff face were also the world's largest standing images of the Buddha images, which were destroyed in early 2001 by the Taliban, the Muslim rulers of Afghanistan at the time. The niches surrounding the two standing Buddhas and the walls of the various grottos were also decorated with Buddhist paintings. These too have been removed over the years; some were destroyed, while others are now housed in private collections and museums around the world.

Historical Background

Located in the Hindu Kush mountains, the Bamiyan valley was traversed by thousands of merchants transporting goods between Central Asia and China, as well as by Buddhist pilgrims journeying to and from northern India. Between the first and third centuries AD, during the reigns of the Kushan king Kanishka and his successors, a system of monastic caves was built into the cliffs northeast of the capital of Bamiyan. During the second to third century AD, the smaller of the two colossal Buddhas (136 feet high) was carved into the cliff face, and roughly a century later the larger one (186 feet high) was constructed. By around 400 AD, the valley of Bamiyan was known for its colossal Buddhas and its monasteries of over 1,000 monks. In the seventh century, the Chinese pilgrim Xuanzang (30) noted the two large Buddhas with their golden hues and their dazzling ornamentation. In the next few centuries, many inhabitants of this region converted to Islam, but the country of Bamiyan remained Buddhist until around the eleventh century, after which Buddhism more or less disappeared from the valley. Devastation of the nearby royal city by the Mongols in the thirteenth century, and a decrease in the amount of overland trade in the region, led to the area's decline. The caves were inhabited by local people, and over time, the faces of the standing Buddhas and others figures were destroyed by Muslims in keeping with their abhorrence of religious idols. The two Buddhas were finally destroyed in 2001.

Main Features

The main features of the cave complex were the two colossal standing Buddhas which dominated the valley. The earlier, smaller Buddha showed the direct influence of Gandharan Buddhist sculptural styles, with its rigid frontal position, heavy proportions and the Greco-Roman approach to drapery (**ill. 2**). The later, larger Buddha had more harmonious physical proportions and showed the influence of newer Indian sculptural traditions (**ill. 3**). Originally both Buddha figures were brightly painted, the larger one red, and the smaller blue. They had gilding on the face and hands and were decorated with ornaments. All around them in the niches were brightly painted images of deities and celestial beings, and images of some of the paintings' patrons.

1 View of the Potala Palace, Lhasa (above)

2 View of buildings within the Potala Palace (left)

3 Roof decoration of two deer flanking the Wheel of the Law (below)

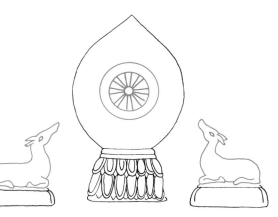

The Potala Palace in Lhasa, Tibet is one of the largest examples of Buddhist architecture. The structure, built in the seventeenth century by the Fifth Dalai Lama, is part monastery, part military fortress, and part administrative centre. It served as the home of the Dalai Lama, and thus the centre of Tibetan government, until 1959, when the Fourteenth Dalai Lama went into exile. The grandeur of this awesome stone building, looming over the lake and plains below, has symbolized to the people of Tibet the unity of spiritual and temporal power represented by the Dalai Lama.

Historical Background

The Potala Palace was originally built by the Fifth Dalai Lama (1617–82), leader of the Gelukpa sect, which gained predominance in Tibet in the first half of the seventeenth century. The 'Great Fifth' consolidated political power in 1642 and, for the first time, the Dalai Lama became the political leader of the Tibetan people. Consequently, the Dalai Lama's sect, the Gelukpa order, became the most powerful religious order in Tibet. In 1645, the Dalai Lama embarked on an extensive building programme, including several major monasteries, and enlarged the former palace of Tibet's first great religious king, Songtsen Gambo, located on Marpori, the 'Red Mountain' overlooking the plains of Lhasa. The final structure, the Potala Palace, was completed in 1695, thirteen years after the Fifth Dalai Lama's death, although his death was kept secret until its completion. The palace was named after Potalaka, a Buddhist paradise (72), or pure land, thought to be located somewhere south of India. This is the pure land of the compassionate bodhisattva Avalokiteshvara (8), of whom the Dalai Lama is believed to be an emanation.

Main Features

In Tibet, most monasteries and homes of spiritual teachers were built in inconspicuous settings. However, the Potala Palace, often considered the foremost monument of distinctly Tibetan architecture, symbolizes the union of the spiritual with the political. Although it was the residence of the country's foremost spiritual teacher, the Potala Palace, with its dramatic hilltop location, owes more to palace or fortress architecture and planning than to any monastic tradition (**ill. 1**). The enormous structure is characterized by high tapering walls extending down the side of the hill and elaborate zig-zag staircases that wind down towards the base of the hill. It is also said to have a total of 1,000 windows (**ill. 2**).

In the central section of the Palace are the red buildings comprising the Potrang Marpo, or 'Red Palace', where religious services are held. The Red Palace is flanked by four chapels, one of which contains the burial stupa of the Fifth Dalai Lama. The roofs of the building are mostly flat and are decorated with symbols such as the Wheel of the Law (42) flanked by two deer (53), representing the Buddha's first sermon at the Deer Park near Sarnath (**ill. 3**). Inside are numerous masterpieces of Tibetan Buddhist art, including wall paintings and sculptures dating back several centuries.

1 Seated Buddha with attendants, stone, 5th century, Longmen caves (left)

2 Seated Vairochana, Fengxian cave temple, 7th century, Longmen caves (right)

3 Guardian figures and bodhisattva, 7th century, Longmen caves (below)

The cave complex at Longmen, just outside the city of Luoyang in Henan province, is one of the most impressive devotional projects undertaken by Buddhist rulers anywhere in Asia. Following the tradition of the great Indian rock cave temples, this temple complex was begun at the end of the fifth century under the patronage of the Northern Wei court (420–534), and was worked on continuously for 400 years under the Buddhist rulers of the Tang dynasty (618–906). Like the Tangyao cave temples of the Northern Wei dynasty at Yungang in Shanxi province (carved 460–93), the Longmen cave complex is made up of a series of large limestone caves temples, in which colossal Buddha figures were carved out of the rock face. The Longmen cave temples provide valuable information about the evolution of Chinese Buddhist artistic styles and iconography. In addition, inscriptions and sculptures of donors illustrate the nature of Buddhist artistic patronage in China over four centuries.

Historical Background

The caves at Longmen were first carved under the patronage of the Northern Wei, a dynasty of Turkish rulers who dominated north China through the fifth and early sixth centuries. The first Buddhist rulers of China, the Northern Wei moved their capital to Luoyang in 494, and began building the Longmen tomb complex as a centre of worship. After the demise of the Northern Wei, the main patrons of the Longmen caves were the Buddhist rulers of the Tang dynasty, including the Emperor Gaozong (ruled 650–83) and his formidable wife, the Empress Wu (ruled 690–705), a devout patron of large-scale Buddhist projects. She was especially interested in the complex rituals and imagery of True Word (Chinese: Zhenyan) esoteric Buddhism, a tradition that virtually disappeared from China at the end of the eighth century, only to be resurrected in Japan as the Shingon school by the Japanese monk, Kobo Daishi (31).

Main Features

The Longmen cave complex features four centuries of Chinese sculptural output. The earliest figures of the Longmen complex are in the traditional Northern Wei style of the fifth century. The Buddha figures are massive, somewhat stiff figures with large heads and hands, gently smiling faces and highly stylized drapery (**ill. 1**). The later caves, however, feature Chinese Buddhist sculpture of a very different style. The Buddha, bodhisattva and guardian figures of the seventh-century Fengxian cave temple, in particular, are depicted in full Tang dynasty style, with fleshier physiques and meditative, almost distant, facial expressions. Their robes fall realistically over their bodies. According to legend, the central Buddha in this cave, the Cosmic Buddha Vairochana (4) bears the facial features of the Empress Wu (**ill. 2**). At the sides, the guardian figures, dressed in Tang dynasty armour and traditional Indian robes, strike dynamic bending poses reminiscent of early Indian sculpture (**ill. 3**). Many East Asian images of guardian kings, in particular, the Four Heavenly Kings (18), are modelled on Tang dynasty guardian figures such as these.

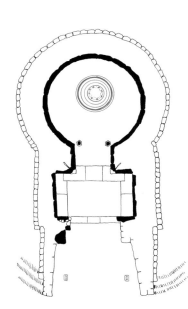

1 Plan of Sokkuram Cave temple (left)

2 Seated Buddha surrounded by relief carvings of monks and bodhisattvas (below)

The small Buddhist monument known as Sokkuram, the 'Stone Cave Hermitage', is one of Korea's most important Buddhist sites and contains some of the finest examples of Buddhist art in stone. Built in the eighth century on Mount T'oham near the ancient Korean capital of Kyongju, this Buddhist shrine was constructed in cut stone in imitation of traditional Indian, Chinese and Central Asian rock-cut cave shrines. Now considered one of Asia's greatest Buddhist monuments, Sokkuram and the nearby temple complex, Pulguksa, the 'Temple of the Buddha Land', were both constructed during the Unified Silla period (668–935), the Golden Age of Korean Buddhism, when Korea was profoundly influenced by the arts and culture of Tang China. Both of these sites were constructed as acts of religious devotion and as demonstrations of political power.

Historical Background

The Pulguksa temple and the Sokkuram shrine were both built by Prime Minister Kim Taesong (700–74) in the second half of the eighth century. The Pulguksa was one of the first Korean Buddhist temples and had existed since the sixth century in the city of Kyongju. Kim Taesong had it rebuilt around 751 in honour of his parents, in a gesture that is at once Buddhist and Confucian since it demonstrated filial piety. The following year, he begun the construction of the Sokkuram cave temple in the hills near the Pulguksa in an attempt to recreate Indian and Chinese cave shrines in a Korean setting. The complex was abandoned, probably in the Choson period (1392–1910), but was rediscovered in a dilapidated state in the twentieth century and was reconstructed by the Japanese using the original pieces.

Main Features

The shrine of Sokkuram is constructed out of granite with a rectangular ante-chamber and a domed main chamber, in imitation of Indian cave temples (**ill. 1**). A seated granite Buddha over 11 feet high, is positioned in the centre of the domed chamber to allow worshippers to circumambulate it (**ill. 2**). The style of the Buddha, carved in the round with a fleshy face and solid physique, closely resembles Tang Chinese examples, with an added Korean softness in the facial expression and the delicacy of the folds of the robes. The figure is generally referred to as the Historical Buddha, Shakyamuni (1), since his right hand reaches over his knee to touch the ground in the earth-touching mudra (43). However, some scholars insist that he is Amitabha (6) Buddha, since he sits facing eastward and is surrounded by certain bodhisattvas and celestial figures that usually accompany Amitabha.

On the walls around the Buddha are forty-one figures of bodhisattvas, deities, guardians and monks carved in relief. Most remarkable is a rare carved image of the Eleven-headed Avalokiteshvara (8) holding a lotus (48) and a water sprinkling vessel (59). Originally, openings in the walls of the shrine allowed light to shine into the shrine and play upon the surface of these statues.

1 The Great Buddha Hall of the Todaiji temple (top)

2 Vairochana, the Cosmic Buddha at the Todaiji (left)

3 Engraving of bodhisattvas on the lotus throne of Vairochana (above)

The Todaiji, the 'Eastern Great Temple', in Nara is one of the most important Buddhist sites in Japan. It was commissioned by Emperor Shomu (ruled 724–49) as a means of protecting the nation under the Buddhist Law, hence its full name, 'Temple for the Protection of the Nation by the Golden Radiant Four Heavenly Kings (18)' (Japanese: Konko Myo Shitenno Gokokuji). Since its construction in the eighth century, the Todaiji has been destroyed by fire several times and then rebuilt on a smaller scale. However, its main hall, the Great Buddha Hall (Daibutsuden) remains the largest wooden structure in the world (**ill. 1**) and contains the largest free-standing bronze statue in the world, the image of Vairochana (4). The temple's construction marked the first significant convergence of church and state in Japan.

Historical Background

Emperor Shomu, Japan's most devoutly Buddhist ruler, was inspired by various Buddhist sutras that equated the power of an earthly ruler with the power of the Buddha. According to certain sutras, the Buddha would protect and assist any king who followed his teachings, and the Four Heavenly Kings would offer their services as guardians of the kingdom. Like Ashoka in India and the Tang Emperor Gaozong of China, Shomu sought to centralize and rule his nation according to Buddhist law. In 741, he issued an edict launching a massive building programme of Buddhist monasteries, or kokubunji, throughout Japan's sixty-seven provinces. The Todaiji in Nara, the capital, was to be the national headquarters and spiritual and political centre of the nation. He also ordered the construction of a 53-feet-high bronze image of Vairochana, which was consecrated in 752 before an international audience, including more than 10,000 monks. The Great Buddha Hall was built around it shortly afterwards. The project took over fifteen years, involved the excavation and landscaping of one side of Mount Wakakusa, several millions of hours of skilled labour, and depleted the nation's supply of copper and tin.

Main Features

The statue and Great Buddha Hall date to the early eighteenth century, but closely follow the original structures. The huge bronze figure of Vairochana, sitting with his right hand in the gesture of fearlessness (41), was originally covered in gold (**ill. 2**). The eighteenth-century statue still sits on its original eighth-century lotus throne (36), the petals of which are engraved with bodhisattvas, guardian figures and paradise scenes (**ill. 3**). Some of the smaller buildings contain many original Nara period sculptures. Some of the most important statues are the figures of the Four Heavenly Kings (Shi Tenno) in the Kaidan'in Hall. These eighth-century figures have fierce facial expressions and wear Chinese suits of armour. The Shosoin, the Imperial Repository of Emperor Shomu, contained thousands of early examples of Buddhist textiles, ritual objects and decorative arts from Japan and overseas. They are now housed in the Nara National Museum.

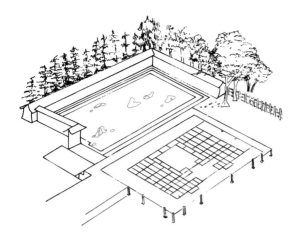

1 Plan of dry garden at Ryoanji (left)

2 Visitors viewing dry garden, Ryoanji (above)

3 View of dry garden, Ryoanji (below)

The Ryoanji, 'Temple of the Peaceful Dragon', is a Zen Buddhist temple located in northwestern Kyoto. Built in the late fifteenth century, the temple is best known for its Zen garden created with rocks and raked gravel. Such dry plantless gardens are known as 'withered mountain and water' (kare-sansui) and are miniature abstracted representations of the natural world. These gardens are not meant to be strolled in, but are viewed like a painting from a number of fixed vantage points along the adjoining verandah. They are used as focal points in certain Zen meditational exercizes. Described as a 'monument to stillness', the Ryoanji garden, with its perfectly arranged rocks rising up from a sea of raked gravel, was created to calm the viewer's mind and induce a sense of nothingness. Practitioners sit in meditation staring at the arrangement with the aim of attaining insight into the nature of the universe (**ill. 2**).

Historical Background

Japan's dry landscape garden tradition began in the Muromachi period (1336–1574), when Japan was ruled by a samurai warrior government based in Kyoto. The samurai were attracted to the simplicity and directness of Zen Buddhist teachings and adopted many Zen practices, including meditation and tea drinking. In 1450, a military figure, Hosokawa Katsumoto, built his residence on the site of an old temple and established the Zen temple of Ryoanji. The temple was destroyed during civil wars, but was rebuilt by his son Hosokawa Masamoto in 1488, and it is generally believed that the dry landscape garden dates to this period. Originally based on Chinese prototypes, these dry gardens were designed initially by Buddhist priests, first from the Shingon tradition and then increasingly from the Zen schools. The creators of the garden at the Ryoanji remain unknown. However, signatures carved on one of the rocks suggest that riverbank workers created the garden with the help of Zen Buddhist monks.

Main Features

The rock and gravel garden of Ryoanji covers an area of 400 square yards on the south side of the temple abbot's headquarters and is bounded by a verandah on its north side and low stone walls to the south (**ill. 1**). The grouped arrangements of seven, five, and three rocks, respectively, are surrounded by areas of raked sand. The larger rocks are placed in the foreground and the smaller ones in the background to create the illusion of perspective and to make the confined space appear larger. Although no plants, trees or water are used, the arrangement of the rocks rising up out of the raked gravel closely resembles a living landscape of groups of islands rising out of the sea (**ill. 3**). Just as in a Zen monochrome ink painting in which the empty space of the white page is as important as the painted image, the empty expanse of raked gravel carries as much weight as the great, looming rocks. Sparse in physical detail, the garden is rich in contrasts: solid form with empty space, and hard, immutable rock with soft, movable gravel. The illusion of seascape is created without water.

Glossary of Key Buddhist Terms

Abhirati (Sanskrit): The Paradise, or **Pure Land,** of the **Buddha** Akshobya (5).

Adi Buddha (Sanskrit): The Primordial **Buddha** who existed before anything else. This infinite, omniscient being created everything, and it is from him that the Five **Dhyani Buddhas** emanate. He is worshipped mainly in Nepal and Tibet.

Ananda: one of the **Buddha**'s chief disciples, charged by the **Buddha** with continuing his teachings.

Arupadhatu (Sanskrit): in the Buddhist cosmos, the Realm of Formlessness and ultimate enlightenment.

asana (Sanskrit): sitting position (38).

Ashoka (ruled 272–231 BC): Emperor of India's Mauryan dynasty (c. 323–185 BC), who converted to Buddhism and promoted the spread of the religion by erecting 84,000 **stupas** (65), writing edicts promoting the **Buddha**'s teachings on pillars.

attribute: identifying object or symbol usually held or worn by a **Buddha, bodhisattva** or deity. Also a physical characteristic.

axis mundi (Latin): literally, the 'pillar of the world'; usually a tree, mountain, pillar or pole that is believed to connect Heaven and Earth.

bhikshu (Sanskrit), **bhikku** (Pali): monk.

bodhi (Sanskrit): **enlightenment,** awakening.

bodhi tree: tree under which the **Buddha** attained **enlightenment;** the tree was a pipal, or *ficus religiosa,* a member of the fig family (51). A descendant of the original bodhi tree is preserved at Bodh Gaya, India (74).

bodhisattva (Sanskrit): being who is destined for **enlightenment,** or **Buddha**hood, but who postpones his or her own **enlightenment** in order to help other beings achieve salvation.

Brahmanism: early form of Indian religion that evolved into Hinduism; priests, known as *brahman,* performed sacrificial rites and had knowledge of the Vedas (sacred texts).

Buddha (Sanskrit): awakened or enlightened being.

Chakravartin (Sanskrit): literally, 'turner of the wheel'; in Indian myth, a world-conquering king whose virtue, earned by good deeds in former lives, gives him the power to subjugate all lesser kings and rule the world.

chaitya (Sanskrit): assembly hall, used by practitioners for group worship.

chan (Chinese): meditation; the name of the Chinese form of meditational Buddhism that became **Zen** Buddhism in Japan. See also **dhyana.**

chorten (Tibetan): see **stupa.**

circumambulation: meditative walking around an object of worship, usually a **stupa** or an image of a **Buddha.**

consort: the female counterpart of a male Buddhist deity. The male represents compassion, while the female consort represents wisdom. The union of these two forces is necessary for the attainment of **enlightenment.**

Daoism (Taoism): ancient Chinese belief system based on the concept of the Dao, or 'Way', a force that engenders and yet permeates all things, and the two opposing yet harmonious forces of yin and yang that activate the universe.

Dalai Lama (Dalai: Mongolian for 'oceanic', Lama: Tibetan for 'spiritual master'): spiritual and political leader of Tibet since 1642, when the fifth Dalai Lama, Losang Gyatso, held secular and spiritual authority over Tibet. Subsequent Dalai Lamas ruled Tibet until 1959, when the Fourteenth Dalai Lama fled into exile.

dharani (Sanskrit): literally, 'that which supports'; a collection of **mantras** or sacred formulas.

dharma (Sanskrit): before the time of the **Buddha,** the Indian term referred to religion, law, duty, or custom, to any pattern that controls human behaviour and thought. The teachings of the **Buddha,** which offer a path towards **enlightenment,** are called the **dharma.**

dhyana (Sanskrit): meditation; the term was translated into Chinese as **chan** and into Japanese as **Zen.**

Dhyani Bodhisattva (Sanskrit): one of the bodhisattvas who corresponds to the **Dhyani Buddhas.**

Dhyani Buddha (Sanskrit): one of the five transcendental **Buddhas** of **Mahayana** and **Vajrayana** Buddhism, also known as **jinas,** 'conquerors', or **tathagatas,** 'those who have gone thus'. These Five Dhyani **Buddhas** exist in the spiritual realm and are often considered to be aspects of the **Buddha,** his various spiritual qualities and his teachings.

Diamond World: the masculine aspect of the Buddhist universe, which corresponds to other Buddhist symbols of the masculine, including the **vajra** and male deities, when embracing their female **shakti**. It is unified with the **Womb World** in the **Mandalas** of the Two Worlds (73).

Dvarapala (Sanskrit): door guardians represented in pairs at the entrance to temples, **stupas** (65), and pagodas, in particular in Java, Indonesia (81).

Eightfold Path: essential teachings of the **Buddha** that help followers overcome desire and attachment: (1) Right View, (2) Right Thought, (3) Right Speech, (4) Right Action, (5) Right Livelihood, (6) Right Effort, (7) Right Awareness, (8) Right Concentration. The first two parts lead to wisdom, the next three are in the realm of behaviour, the final three relate to meditation.

enlightenment: goal of most Buddhist practitioners; the perfection of wisdom, the direct understanding of the true nature of reality, and its result, compassion for others and freedom from suffering.

Esoteric Buddhism: see **Vajrayana Buddhism.**

Four Noble Truths: core of the **Buddha**'s teachings, and the truth about reality that he understood at the point of **enlightenment**: (1) in all life, there is suffering; (2) the cause of suffering is desire or attachment; (3) to end suffering, one must overcome desire and attachment; (4) to overcome desire and attachment, one must follow the **Eightfold Path.**

Gelukpa (Tibetan): Tibetan Buddhist sect founded by the main disciples of Tsong Khapa. Its followers are distinguishable by their yellow hats. It became the country's most powerful order in the seventeenth century. The **Dalai Lama** is their leader.

Goddess of Mercy: common name given by Europeans to the compassionate **bodhisattva** Avalokiteshvara (8), particularly in East Asia, where depictions of this **bodhisattva** are often feminine and may be shown as maternal figures carrying small children.

guru (Sanskrit): teacher or spiritual guide.

Hinayana (Sanskrit): literally, 'Lesser Vehicle', a term coined by the **Mahayana** Buddhists to refer to the **Southern Schools** of monastic Buddhism, including the **Theravada** tradition, that spread via southern India to Southeast Asia; it stresses the salvation of the individual.

Hinduism: complex religious and social tradition that grew in India over thousands of years. Fundamental to Hindus is the idea of moksha (like the Buddhist **nirvana**), the release of the soul from the perpetual cycle of rebirth, **samsara**. Hindus believe that the accumulation of good **karma** can lead to a higher rebirth and ultimate release. The numerous Hindu gods can also assist Hindus towards salvation.

Jainism: Indian religion that, like Buddhism, evolved in the sixth century BC as a reaction to Hinduism. The goal of Jains is to perfect their souls and release them from the cycle of rebirth (**samsara**). Many practise non-violence and strict asceticism as a means of perfecting their souls. Perfected beings are known as **jinas** (conquerors), or Tirthankaras (crossing-builders). These beings are very similar to **Buddhas.**

jatakas (Sanskrit): episodes from the former lives of the **Buddha**. These morality tales communicate proper behaviour to followers to help them accumulate good **karma** and achieve a favourable rebirth.

Jambudvipa (Sanskrit): name of the Indian subcontinent in Indian cosmology.

Jayavarman VII (ruled 1181–1219): Cambodia's foremost Buddhist monarch, responsible for Buddhist projects including Angkor Thom.

jina (Sanskrit): literally 'conqueror'; see **Dhyani Buddha.**

Kagyupa (Tibetan): Tibetan Buddhist order founded by Marpa, with more mystical teachings than the other orders. Several other sects branched off from this order, including the Drukpa, the Karmapa, and the Talungpa.

Kamadhatu (Sanskrit): the realm of desire, one of the spheres in Buddhist cosmology.

karma (Sanskrit): literally 'action' or 'deed'; the accumulation of good or bad karma dictates the level at which one's soul will be reborn.

karuna (Sanskrit): compassion. In **Mahayana** and **Vajrayana** thought, this force must unite with wisdom, or **prajna**, for **enlightenment** to be possible.

kare sansui (Japanese): dry landscape garden, made with rocks and gravel, found particularly in Japan's **Zen** Buddhist temples.

Kim Taesong (700–774): Korean Prime Minister who commissioned important Buddhist sites including the Pulguksa and the Sokkuram temples (86).

kirtimukkha (Sanskrit): literally 'face of glory'; demonic mask placed over doorways and windows, originated in India but best known in Java.

koan (Japanese): unsolvable conundrum posed to **Zen** trainees to ponder during meditation, such as, 'What is the sound of one hand clapping?' The quality of the student's response indicates the trainee's level of understanding.

kshatriya (Sanskrit): member of the warrior class in traditional Indian society; one level below the brahman class. Shakyamuni (1) was a member of this class.

lakshana (Sanskrit): auspicious attributes or marks on the body of the **Buddha** – e.g., **ushnisha**, **urna**, etc. (33).

lama (Tibetan): religious or spiritual master; leader of a Tibetan Buddhist community. The term can also be used for any Tibetan monk.

The Law: philosophical teachings of the **Buddha**; also known as the **dharma**.

Lokapala (Sanskrit): literally 'guardians of the world', protecting the four cardinal directions (18).

Lotus Sutra: known in Sanskrit as the *Saddharma Pundarika Sutra*, this major Mahayana text stresses the idea of the one, eternal, omniscient **Buddha** presiding over all things. It also claims that all believers can attain **Buddha**hood, so found particular favour with women. The important twenty-fifth chapter describes the infinite compassion of Avalokiteshvara (8).

Mahayana Buddhism: literally, the 'Great Vehicle'; also known as the Universal Vehicle, as it stresses universal salvation, rather than the salvation of the individual. It is practised mainly in China, Korea, and Japan. It emerged in the first century AD and is distinct from the older, more orthodox **Hinayana** traditions including **Theravada**. This tradition emphasizes the role of the **bodhisattva**, who postpones his own **enlightenment** in order to help others. It also teaches that compassion is as important a virtue as wisdom.

makara (Sanskrit): mythical animal (54), part crocodile, part elephant, used in Buddhist and Hindu temples above doorways.

mandala (Sanskrit): literally a 'sacred space that has been set aside or adorned'; a geometric diagram that portrays the perfected world of a deity or group of deities (73).

mani (Sanskrit): jewel (49).

mantra (Sanskrit): powerful syllable, word or phrase

recited as a form of meditation, usually associated with a specific deity.

Mara (Sanskrit): evil demon who attempted to prevent **Siddhartha Gautama** (1) from attaining **enlightenment**.

Maya (Sanskrit): illusion; also the name of the mother of the **Buddha** (1).

The Middle Way: philosophy of moderation preached by the **Buddha**, after experiencing two extremes in his own life, the luxurious life of a prince and the harsh life of an ascetic. At the heart of this philosophy is the **Eightfold Path**, which is meant to guide followers along the Middle Way.

Mount Meru: sacred mountain at the centre of the Hindu, Jain, and Buddhist cosmos (52).

mudra (Sanskrit): hand gesture with symbolic meaning used by **Buddhas**, **bodhisattvas**, deities, and Buddhist practitioners; also used in Indian dance (41–44).

naga (Sanskrit): snake or serpent.

Nagarjuna: South Indian philosopher and reformer of Buddhism; lived around the first or second century AD. Most important advocate of the Madhyamika school of Buddhist philosophy.

Nichiren Buddhism (Japanese): Japanese Buddhist school based on the teachings of the controversial thirteenth century monk Nichiren. He stressed the importance of the **Lotus Sutra** as the perfect exposition of truth.

nirvana (Sanskrit): **enlightenment**; the release from the cycle of rebirth, or **samsara**.

Northern Buddhism: term used to describe the Mahayana and Vajrayana schools of Buddhism which spread out of India along a northern route.

Nyingmapa (Tibetan): literally the 'Ancient Order'; a Tibetan Buddhist order founded in the tenth or eleventh centuries by combining various older sects and traditions.

om (Sanskrit): ancient mystical syllable that represents the entirety of the universe. It is an important syllable in many **mantras**, or sacred formulas addressed to Buddhist deities.

Pali: scholarly language from southern India; the main language used in **Hinayana** Buddhist texts.

parinirvana (Sanskrit): literally 'final nirvana'; the final

enlightenment of the **Buddha**, when he died and gave up his corporeal form.

Pitaka (Sanskrit): literally, a 'basket'; body of texts in the **Pali** scriptures of the **Theravada** school. There are three baskets of texts, the **Tripitaka** (Sanskrit) or the **Tipitaka** (Pali).

Potalaka (Sanskrit): the Paradise, or **Pure Land** (72), of the **bodhisattva** Avalokiteshvara (8).

Prajna (Sanskrit): insight or wisdom. In **Mahayana** and **Vajrayana** thought, it must be united with compassion, or **karuna**, for **enlightenment** to be possible.

Prajnaparamita (Sanskrit: perfection of wisdom) **Sutra**: the perfection of wisdom is an understanding of the concept of **shunyata**, or nothingness, which is central to **Mahayana** Buddhist thought. This **sutra** can be 100,000 verses long, but a shortened version, the *Heart Sutra*, is only a few lines long.

puja (Sanskrit): worship or ritual offering to gods, **Buddhas**, or other beings.

Pure Land: paradise, or perfect realm, of a **Buddha** or **bodhisattva**; for example, Amitabha's (6) Pure Land in the West. Also a Chinese and Japanese school of Buddhism that promises worshippers rebirth in Amitabha's Western Pure Land (72).

raigo (Japanese): illustration of Amitabha (6) and his attendants approaching to receive and welcome the soul of the deceased to Paradise.

Rupadhatu (Sanskrit): in the Buddhist cosmos, the Celestial Realm.

samadhi (Sanskrit): deep concentration, a state in which the mind is totally focussed.

samsara (Sanskrit): the endless cycle, of birth, death and rebirth, to which souls are chained; **enlightenment** in the Buddhist context means release from samsara.

samvara: see Yidams (22).

Sangha (Sanskrit): community of Buddhist monks and nuns and, by extension, lay initiates and practitioners.

Sarnath: location of the Deer Park where the **Buddha** gave his first sermon after attaining **enlightenment**. Near Varanasi in modern Uttar Pradesh, India.

satori (Japanese): **enlightenment** in the Japanese Zen tradition, in the sense of perception of one's innate **Buddha**-nature. This **enlightenment** may happen suddenly during one's lifetime.

Seven Lucky Gods: see **Shichifukujin**.

shakti (Sanskrit): female principle or energy, in Hinduism; the female counterpart or consort of a Buddhist deity is often known as his shakti.

Shichifukujin (Japanese), **Seven Lucky Gods**: Japanese folk gods, several deriving from Buddhist deities. Mahakala is Daikoku, God of Wealth. Vaishravana is Bishamonten, God of Good Fortune, and Sarasvati is Benzaiten, Goddess of Learning. The others are the gods of wealth, Ebisu and Hotei, and the gods of longevity, Fukurokuju and Jurojin.

shikhara (Sanskrit): narrow pyramid-shaped element of Hindu architecture used in some Buddhist monuments.

Shingon (Japanese): literally, 'true word'; one of the two Japanese esoteric schools of Buddhism, characterized by rituals and complex speculative doctrines, brought to Japan in the early ninth century by Kobo Daishi (31).

Shomu, Emperor (ruled 724–749): Japan's foremost Buddhist ruler, who patronized the construction of the Todaiji in Nara (86) and unified church and state.

shunyata (Sanskrit): Nothingness or Emptiness; the **Mahayana Buddhist** absolute.

Siddhartha Gautama: Indian prince who later attained **enlightenment** and became the **Buddha**, Shakyamuni (1).

siddhi (Sanskrit): **enlightenment**; miraculous powers; perfection.

Southern Buddhism: the older, monastic schools of Buddhism, often called **Hinayana** by the **Mahayanists**, which travelled to southern India and then to Southeast Asia. Of the **Hinayana** schools, the most enduring has been the **Theravada** school, which still flourishes in Sri Lanka and Southeast Asia.

stupa (Sanskrit): funerary mound or reliquary, often the central feature of a Buddhist temple.

sutra (Sanskrit): from the Sanskrit 'to sew'; a sacred Buddhist text.

tantra (Sanskrit): literally, 'thread' or 'loom'; traditional Indian mystical texts dating from around the seventh century AD. Both Hinduism and Buddhism have well established Tantric traditions based on these texts. Tantra is important in Tibetan Buddhism and involves the use of **mantras**, meditation, **yoga**, and ritual.

Tantric Buddhism: see **Vajrayana Buddhism**.

tathagata (Sanskrit): literally, 'one who has gone thus'; a **Buddha**, or enlightened being. See **Dhyani Buddha**.

thangka (Tibetan): Tibetan scroll painting on cloth that can be rolled up. Most thangkas depict Buddhist deities, Buddhist paradises (72), or **mandalas** (73).

Theravada Buddhism (Sanskrit): literally, the 'School of the Elders'; one of the few surviving early **Hinayana** schools of Buddhism that stressed monasticism, the importance of the holy texts, and meditation. This ancient, orthodox school of Buddhism is practised today in Sri Lanka, Burma, Thailand, Cambodia, and Laos.

torana (Sanskrit): gateway or entranceway to a shrine, temple or **stupa**.

tribangha (Sanskrit): literally, 'three bends'; a pose used in Indian sculpture, in which the body bends gracefully at the neck and the hips.

Tripitaka (Sanskrit), **Tipitaka** (Pali): teachings of the **Theravada** tradition of **Hinayana** Buddhism, drawn together in 'triple basket': **sutras** (Sanskrit) or *suttas* (Pali), sacred texts; the *Vinaya* (Rules of the Monastery); and the *Abhidharma* (Sanskrit) or *Abhidamma* (Pali), further teaching.

Triratna (Sanskrit): literally, 'three jewels', referring to the three treasures of Buddhism: the **Buddha**, the teachings (**dharma**), and the monastic community (**sangha**).

Tushita (Sanskrit): heaven where future **Buddhas** dwell, awaiting the right time to appear in this world.

ushnisha (Sanskrit): protrusion on the **Buddha**'s head, signifying his wisdom; one of the thirty-two marks of the **Buddha** (33).

urna (Sanskrit): curled tuft of hair, or third eye, between the eyes of the **Buddha**; one of the thirty-two marks of the **Buddha** (33).

vajra: diamond or thunderbolt (55). The most important symbol of **Vajrayana Buddhism**, it is a short metal weapon of unmatched sharpness, and which possesses the irresistible force of a thunderbolt.

Vajraghanta (Sanskrit): combination of the **vajra** (55) and the bell (58), symbolizing the union of wisdom and compassion.

Vajrayana Buddhism: literally, 'the diamond or thunderbolt vehicle'; also known as Tantrayana, or **Tantric Buddhism**, this esoteric school of Buddhism is mainly practised in Tibet, Nepal and by followers of

Shingon Buddhism in Japan.

vidya (Sanskrit): knowledge.

vihara (Sanskrit): monastery, but within the Indian monastic complex, it is usually applied to the residence halls of monks, as distinct from **chaitya** halls.

Vulture Peak: hill on which the **Buddha** gave many sermons after attaining **enlightenment**. The **Lotus Sutra** is based on some of his sermons at this spot.

Womb World: the feminine aspect of the Buddhist universe, which corresponds to other Buddhist symbols of the feminine, including the **shakti**, the bell and the lotus. It is unified with the **Diamond World** in the **Mandalas** of the Two Worlds (73).

Wrathful deities: Fierce forms assumed by **bodhisattva**s and deities to conquer the evil forces of the universe.

Wu, Empress (ruled 690–705 AD): Chinese empress, probably the foremost female patron of Buddhism and Buddhist arts. Patronized large-scale Buddhist architectural projects, notably the Longmen Caves (84).

Wutaishan (Chinese): the 'Five-peaked Mountain' in China's Shanxi province where Manjushri (12) is believed to reside.

yab-yum (Tibetan): literally, 'father-mother'; position of sexual union representing the union of compassion and wisdom.

yana (Sanskrit): way, vehicle.

yoga (Sanskrit): literally, 'yoke' or 'union'; a spiritual system, common to both **Hinduism** and Buddhism, which uses rigorous physical and mental discipline to effect union with the universal consciousness or spirit.

zazen (Japanese): formal meditation in a sitting position (38).

Zen (Japanese): from the Sanskrit **dhyana**, meaning meditation, Japanese meditational form of Buddhism that emphasizes the teacher-disciple relationship, meditation, and the use of conundrums to induce **enlightenment**.

Further Reading

Buddhism: History and Teachings

Boisselier, Jean, *The Wisdom of the Buddha*, London: Thames & Hudson, 1994

Ch'en, Kenneth, *Buddhism in China: A Historical Survey*, Princeton: Princeton University Press, 1964

De Bary, William Theodore (ed.), *The Buddhist Tradition in India, China and Japan*, New York: Vintage Books, 1972

Ray, Reginald A., *Indestructible Truth: The Living Spirituality of Tibetan Buddhism*, Boston/London: Shambhala, 2000

Scheck, Frank Rainer and Manfred Görgens, *Buddhism*, New York: Barron's Educational Series, Inc., 1999

Shearer, Alistair, *Buddha: The Intelligent Heart*, London: Thames & Hudson, Limited, 1992

Snelling, John, *The Buddhist Handbook: A Complete Guide to Buddhist Teaching and Practice*, London: Rider, 1987

Thurman, Robert A. F., *Essential Tibetan Buddhism*, San Francisco: Harper San Francisco, 1995

Buddhist Art and Iconography

Cummings, Joe, *Buddhist Stupas in Asia: The Shape of Perfection*, Footscray, Victoria: Lonely Planet, 2001

Fisher, Robert E., *Buddhist Art and Architecture*, London: Thames & Hudson, 1993

Frédéric, Louis, *Buddhism: Flammarion Iconographic Guides*, Paris/New York: Flammarion, 1995

Getty, Alice, *The Gods of Northern Buddhism: Their History and Iconography*, New York: Dover Publications, Inc., 1928, 1988

Pal, Pratapaditya, *Light of Asia: Buddha Sakyamuni in Asian Art*, Los Angeles: Los Angeles County Museum of Art, 1984

Rinpoche, Dagyab, *Buddhist Symbols in Tibetan Culture*, Somerville: Wisdom Publications, 1995

Rowland, Benjamin (Jr.), *The Evolution of the Buddha Image*, New York: The Asia Society/ Abrams, 1963

Snellgrove, David L., *The Image of the Buddha*, New York/Tokyo/Paris/ San Francisco: Unesco/ Kodansha International, 1978

Zwalf, W. (ed.), *Buddhism: Art and Faith*, London: British Museum Publications, 1985

Buddhist Art: Tibet, Nepal and Central Asia

Fisher, Robert E., *Art of Tibet*, London: Thames & Hudson, 1997

Leidy, Denise Patry and Robert A. F. Thurman, *Mandala: The Architecture of Enlightenment*, New York: Asia Society Galleries, Tibet House, Boston: Shambhala, 1998

Levenson, Claude B., *Symbols of Tibetan Buddhism*, New York: Assouline, 2000

Mikhail Piotrovsky, *Lost Empire of the Silk Road: Buddhist Art from Khara Khoto*, Milan: Electa, 1993

Pal, Pratapaditya, *Art of the Himalayas: Treasures from Tibet and Nepal*, New York: Hudson Press in Association with the American Federation of Arts, 1991

————, *Art of Nepal*, Berkeley, Los Angeles, London: Los Angeles County Museum of Art in association with University of California Press, 1985

————, *Art of Tibet*, Berkeley, Los Angeles, London: Los Angeles County Museum of Art in association with University of California Press, 1983

Rhie, Marylin M. and Robert A. F. Thurman, *Wisdom and Compassion: The Sacred Art of Tibet*, New York: Asian Art Museum of San Francisco and Tibet House, New York in association with Harry N. Abrams, Inc., 1991

Buddhist Art: East Asia

Fontein, Jan, and Hickman, Money L., *Zen Paintings and Calligraphy*, Boston: Museum of Fine Arts, 1970

ten Grotenhuis, Elizabeth, *Japanese Mandalas: Representations of Sacred Geography*, Honolulu: University of Hawai'i Press, 1999

Little, Stephen, *Visions of the Dharma: Japanese Buddhist Paintings and Prints in the Honolulu Academy of Arts*, Honolulu: University of Hawai'i Press, 1991

McArthur, Meher, *Japanese Buddhist and Shinto Prints: From the Collection of Manly P. Hall*, London: Sam Fogg, 1996

Nishikawa Kyotaro and Sano, Emily J. Sano, *The Great Age of Japanese Buddhist Sculpture: AD 600–1300*, Fort Worth: Kimbell Art Museum/Japan Society, 1982

Weidner, Marsha (ed.), *Latter Days of the Law: Images of Chinese Buddhism 850–1850*, Spencer Museum of Art, University of Kansas in association with University of Hawai'i Press, 1994

Whitfield, Roderick, and Farrer, Anne, *Caves of the Thousand Buddhas: Chinese Art from the Silk Road*, London: British Museum, 1990

Buddhist Art: Southeast Asia

Brown, Robert (ed.), *Art from Thailand*, Mumbai: Marg Publications, 1999

van Beek, Steve and Invernizzi Tettoni, Luca, *The Arts of Thailand*, Hong Kong: Periplus, 1985, 1991

Philip Rawson, *The Art of Southeast Asia*, London/New York: Thames & Hudson, 1967

Stadtner, Donald M. (ed.), *The Art of Burma: New Studies*, Mumbai: Marg Publications, 1999

Illustration
Acknowledgments

All line drawings and maps are by Carol Fulton.
Key: (a) above, (b) below, (t) top, (c) centre, (l) left, and (r) right.

2 (opposite title page) Pacific Asia Museum, Pasadena, CA, Gift of David Kamansky

10 Photo courtesy Alan McArthur

14 Photo courtesy Sandra Sheckter

16 Photo courtesy Alan McArthur

18 (a) Photo courtesy Alan Bair; (b) Courtesy Pacific Asia Museum, Pasadena, CA, Gift of Neil Kreitman

21 Courtesy Pacific Asia Museum, Pasadena, CA, Gift of David Kamansky

22 (a, b) Photo courtesy the author

23 Photo courtesy the author

26 (l) Norton Simon Collection, Pasadena CA; (r) Courtesy David Humphrey

29 (a, b) Photos courtesy Alan McArthur

30 (b) Courtesy the author

32 (l) Norton Simon Collection, Pasadena, CA; (r) Courtesy Pacific Asia Museum, Pasadena, CA, Museum Purchase

34 (a, b) Courtesy Mr Tsunemitsu Yajima, Monya Art Co. Ltd

36 (l) Los Angeles County Museum of Art, From the Nasli and Alice Heeramaneck Collection, purchased with funds provided by the Jane and Justin Dart Foundation; (r) Photo courtesy Bill and Pat Johnston

38 (a) Courtesy Sam Fogg, London; (b) Courtesy Mr Tsunemitsu Yajima, Monya Art Co. Ltd

40 Courtesy Pacific Asia Museum, Pasadena, CA, Gift of Mr and Mrs Joseph Kamansky

42 (al) Courtesy Pacific Asia Museum, Pasadena, CA, Gift of Mrs Lawrence Shepard; (bl) Photo courtesy Alan McArthur, London; (r) Courtesy Sam Fogg, London

44 (l) Courtesy Pacific Asia Museum, Pasadena, CA, Gift of Mr and Mrs Robert M. Snukal; (b) Courtesy Pacific Asia Museum, Pasadena, CA, Gift of Patricia Ayers Gallucci; (r) Courtesy Pacific Asia Museum, Pasadena, CA, Gift of David Uyematsu

46 (l) The Norton Simon Foundation, Pasadena, CA; (b) Courtesy Pacific Asia Museum, Pasadena , CA, Gift of Mr Louis O. Widner, Sr

50 (a, bl) Courtesy Sam Fogg, London; (br) Photo courtesy the author

52 (br)Courtesy the author

54 Courtesy Mr Tsunemitsu Yajima, Monya Art Co. Ltd

56 (l) Courtesy Pacific Asia Museum, Pasadena, CA, Gift from the Nancy King Collection; (r) Los Angeles County Museum of Art, From the Nasli and Alice Heeramaneck Collection, Museum Associates Purchase

58 (l) Courtesy Pacific Asia Museum, Pasadena, CA, Gift from the Nancy King Collection; (r) Courtesy Pacific Asia Museum, Pasadena, CA, Gift of Dr and Mrs Jesse Greenstein

60 (l) Courtesy Mr Tsunemitsu Yajima, Monya Art Co. Ltd; (r) Courtesy Pacific Asia Museum, Pasadena, CA, Gift of Dr and Mrs Jesse Greenstein

62 Photo courtesy Ruth Hayward

66 (al) Courtesy the Ruth and Sherman Lee Institute for Japanese Art at the Clark Center, Hanford, California; (r, bl) Courtesy Pacific Asia Museum, Pasadena, CA, Gift from the Nancy King Collection

68 Photo courtesy the author

70 (l, r) Courtesy Mr Tsunemistu Yajima, Monya Art. Co., Ltd

72 Santa Barbara Museum of Art, Gift of F. Bailey Vanderhoef, Jr.

74 (l) Courtesy Pacific Asia Museum, Pasadena, CA, Museum Purchase

76 Courtesy Pacific Asia Museum, Pasadena, CA, Gift of the Hon. and Mrs Jack Lydman

78 (l) Courtesy Pacific Asia Museum, Pasadena, CA, Estate of Mr and Mrs Wilmont Gordon; (r) Courtesy Pacific Asia Museum, Pasadena, CA, Gift of David Uyematsu

82 (r) Courtesy Pacific Asia Museum, Pasadena, CA, Gift of Mr and Mrs Robert Nordskog; (l) Courtesy David Kamansky

84 (l) Courtesy Mr Tsunemitsu Yajima, Monya Art Co. Ltd; (b) Courtesy Pacific Asia Museum Store, Pasadena, CA; (r) Courtesy Pacific Asia Museum, Pasadena, CA, Gift of Dr and Mrs Calvin Frazier

86 (l) Courtesy Pacific Asia Museum, Pasadena, CA; (r) Los Angeles County Museum of Art, Gift of Dr and Mrs Pratapaditya Pal in memory of Christian Humann

88 (r) Courtesy Mr Tsunemitsu Yajima, Monya Art. Co. Ltd; (l) Courtesy Pacific Asia Museum, Pasadena, CA, Gift from the Nancy King Collection

90 (r) Courtesy Sam Fogg, London; (l) Courtesy Tom Grayson

92 (l) Photo courtesy Alan McArthur; (r) Courtesy Pacific Asia Museum, Pasadena, CA, Gift of Robert Bentley

94 Courtesy Leslie Rinchen Wongmo

96 (l) Courtesy Pacific Asia Museum, Pasadena, CA, Gift of Mr Paul Sherbert; (ar) Courtesy Pacific Asia Museum, Pasadena, CA, Gift of Edward Nagel; (br) Courtesy Pacific Asia Museum, Pasadena, CA, Gift of Blanche Pope in memory of Edkar Pope

98 (a) Courtesy Leslie Rinchen Wongmo; (b) Photo courtesy Alan McArthur

100 (l) Photo courtesy Pacific Asia Museum, Pasadena, CA, Gift of David Uyematsu; (r) Courtesy Mr Tsunemitsu Yajima, Monya Art Co., Ltd

102 (l) Courtesy Pacific Asia Museum, Pasadena, CA, Estate of Lily Laub; (r) Courtesy Pacific Asia Museum, Pasadena, CA, Gift from the Nancy King Collection

104 (l) Photo courtesy Alan McArthur; (ar) Courtesy Pacific Asia Museum, Pasadena, CA, Gift of Mr and Mrs Joseph Kamansky; (br) Courtesy Pacific Asia Museum, Pasadena, CA, Gift from the Nancy King Collection

106 (a) Courtesy Sam Fogg, London; (b) Photo courtesy Alan McArthur

108 Courtesy Pacific Asia Museum, Pasadena, CA, Gift from the Nancy King Collection

110 (l, r) Courtesy Pacific Asia Museum, Pasadena, CA, Gift from the Nancy King Collection

112 (l) Courtesy Pacific Asia Museum, Pasadena, CA, Gift from the Nancy King Collection; (r) The Norton Simon Foundation, Pasadena, CA

114 (a, b) Photo courtesy Alan McArthur

116 (a) Courtesy Mr Tsunemitsu Yajima, Monya Art Co., Ltd; (b) Courtesy Pacific Asia Museum, Pasadena, CA, Gift of Anna and Dana Bresnahan

120 Photos by John C. Huntington, compliments of The Huntington Archive

122 (a) Courtesy Pacific Asia Museum, Gift of Robert Bentley; (b) Photo courtesy Tools for Peace, Los Angeles

124 (ar, al) Photo courtesy the author; (c) Courtesy Leslie Rinchen Wongmo

126 (l) Courtesy Leslie Rinchen Wongmo; (r) Courtesy the Ruth and Sherman Lee Institute for Japanese Art and the Clark Center, Hanford, California.

128 (a) Courtesy Pacific Asia Museum, Pasadena, CA, Gift of Mr Wiliam Atwood in memory of Elain Spaulding Atwood; (bl) Courtesy Pacific Asia Museum, Pasadena, CA, Gift of Daniel Ostroff; (br)

Index

Page numbers in **bold** refer to illustrations.